Editor-in-Chief and Founder:
  Lyndon H. LaRouche, Jr.
Editorial Board: *Lyndon H. LaRouche, Jr. , Helga
  Zepp-LaRouche, Robert Ingraham, Tony
  Papert, Gerald Rose, Dennis Small, Jeffrey
  Steinberg, William Wertz*
Co-Editors: *Robert Ingraham, Tony Papert*
Technology: *Marsha Freeman*
Books: *Katherine Notley*
Ebooks: *Richard Burden*
Graphics: *Alan Yue*
Photos: *Stuart Lewis*
Circulation Manager: *Stanley Ezrol*

INTELLIGENCE DIRECTORS
Counterintelligence: *Jeffrey Steinberg, Michele
  Steinberg*
Economics: *John Hoefle, Marcia Merry Baker,
  Paul Gallagher*
History: *Anton Chaitkin*
Ibero-America: *Dennis Small*
Russia and Eastern Europe: *Rachel Douglas*
United States: *Debra Freeman*

INTERNATIONAL BUREAUS
Bogotá: *Miriam Redondo*
Berlin: *Rainer Apel*
Copenhagen: *Tom Gillesberg*
Houston: *Harley Schlanger*
Lima: *Sara Madueño*
Melbourne: *Robert Barwick*
Mexico City: *Gerardo Castilleja Chávez*
New Delhi: *Ramtanu Maitra*
Paris: *Christine Bierre*
Stockholm: *Ulf Sandmark*
United Nations, N.Y.C.: *Leni Rubinstein*
Washington, D.C.: *William Jones*
Wiesbaden: *Göran Haglund*

ON THE WEB
e-mail: eirns@larouchepub.com
www.larouchepub.com
www.executiveintelligencereview.com
www.larouchepub.com/eiw
Webmaster: *John Sigerson*
Assistant Webmaster: *George Hollis*
Editor, Arabic-language edition: *Hussein Askary*

EIR (ISSN 0273-6314) *is published weekly
(50 issues), by EIR News Service, Inc.,
P.O. Box 17390, Washington, D.C. 20041-0390.
(703) 297-8434*

European Headquarters: E.I.R. GmbH, Postfach
Bahnstrasse 9a, D-65205, Wiesbaden, Germany
Tel: 49-611-73650
Homepage: http://www.eir.de
e-mail: info@eir.de
Director: Georg Neudecker

Montreal, Canada: 514-461-1557
eir@eircanada.ca

Denmark: EIR - Danmark, Sankt Knuds Vej 11,
basement left, DK-1903 Frederiksberg, Denmark.
Tel.: +45 35 43 60 40, Fax: +45 35 43 87 57. e-mail:
eirdk@hotmail.com.

Mexico City: EIR, Sor Juana Inés de la Cruz 242-2
Col. Agricultura C.P. 11360
Delegación M. Hidalgo, México D.F.
Tel. (5525) 5318-2301
eirmexico@gmail.com

Copyright: ©2017 EIR News Service. All rights
reserved. Reproduction in whole or in part without
permission strictly prohibited.

Canada Post Publication Sales Agreement
#40683579

Postmaster: Send all address changes to *EIR*, P.O.
Box 17390, Washington, D.C. 20041-0390.

Signed articles in *EIR* represent the views of the authors,
and not necessarily those of the Editorial Board.

Beginning of the End of the Coup?

EIRContents

www.larouchepub.com Volume 45, Number 5, February 2, 2018

Cover This Week

Robert Mueller

FBI

BEGINNING OF THE END OF THE COUP?

I. Strategic Directions

II. The New Silk Road Envelops the World

III. The Creative Individual and Economic Progress

ZEPP-LAROUCHE WEBCAST

Our Opportunity at This Moment To Change History Forever

Helga Zepp-LaRouche's weekly webcast of Jan. 25 can be seen at newparadigm.schillerinstitute.com. This transcript has been edited.

Harley Schlanger: Hello! I'm Harley Schlanger from the Schiller Institute. Welcome to this week's Schiller Institute international webcast, featuring the founder of the Schiller Institutes and President of the German Schiller Institute, Helga Zepp-LaRouche.

This has been another week of extremely fast-paced developments, from the Swiss Alps to the Pacific region, through Latin America, and I think it's crucial that we evaluate where we stand now with the State of the Union address coming in the United States next week, and President Trump speaking in Davos tomorrow.

Helga, there were some very strong financial warnings at Davos, even while the global elite seem to be celebrating this fake news of the great global economic recovery. What's the real story?

Helga Zepp-LaRouche: William White, the former chief economist of the Bank for International Settlements, who is now in a leading position in the OECD, gave a very interesting interview to Ambrose Evans-Pritchard from the British *Daily Telegraph*, warning that the next financial crash is inevitable. Now, I think this is absolutely true. We have said it many times, but it's good to hear it from at least one prominent economist. He blames "quantitative easing" for that coming crash, saying that this policy of pumping out money has created a "Catch-22" situation, since the central banks really cannot continue

forever with the zero interest rate policy and quantitative easing. There are already very clear global inflationary pressures. That just makes the bubble bigger. The longer you wait, the worse it becomes, until it finally explodes.

On the other hand, if they want to end that, which they do—then even the slightest increase in the interest rate could trigger a crash. And White pointed to the fact that there are many fracture points in the global financial system. He said in effect that the crash is inevitable.

Now that is obviously a subject which is so grave that it deserves full attention at the Davos World Economic Forum, because somewhere around 2,500 to

courtesy of Institute for New Economic Thinking

William White, Chairman of the Economic Development and Review Committee of the Organization for Economic Co-operation and Development (OECD).

3,000 top bankers, government officials, and corporate CEOs, are there. You would think that they would have to come up with solutions.

But the speeches made so far—including German Chancellor Merkel, Indian Prime Minister Modi, and French President Macron—all said various things, but nothing to address this fundamental question.

The one exception was the Chinese representative Liu He, a key advisor to President Xi Jinping and a new member of the Political Bureau. He is said to be probably the most influential advisor to Xi Jinping concerning the structural reforms inside China and gave a decent speech warning of the problems in the financial system.

In German, there is a proverb which goes *"ausser Spesen nichts gewesen"*; I don't know if this exists in English, but it means that other than a lot of bills to be paid, nothing much is coming out of this Davos meeting. So, I think the problems really remain, and unless Trump, who is supposed to speak tomorrow, makes a miracle speech—which I don't think is to be expected—this meeting will come to an end without solving the urgent financial crisis.

And just to add to the insanity of this, you have so-called economists like Professor Kenneth Rogoff from Harvard, who says "Yes, the next financial crisis will be centered in China and China will be the trigger point." Nothing could be further from the truth. The Chinese economy is the only sound one, it's unbelievably efficient—it's quick, it's modern, it moves with speed, it's pulling other countries into the Belt and Road Initiative—so it's the only sound, real economic dynamic on the planet. It just shows you that the blame-game is on, but the willingness to go to the root of the problem, which would require Glass-Steagall and a Hamiltonian banking system that we have been organizing for—was missing.

Schlanger: One of the points that William White has been making is that you have a number of "zombie companies" that have been kept afloat by means of low interest rates or zero interest rates. They need all the liquidity they can get just to cover the interest on their debt. That's part of the unsustainability. We're seeing some of these companies blow out, like Carillion in Britain, which could lead to 50,000 layoffs!

Now, Helga, the other thing that I think characterizes the urgency of the strategic situation is the report that Robert Mueller, the "legal assassin," is moving to

Senator Chuck Grassley, Iowa, Chairman of the U.S. Senate Judiciary Committee.

get some kind of obstruction of justice charges, clearly a defensive reaction to the explosion of evidence of the corruption of his own staff. What's the latest you have on that?

Zepp-LaRouche: This is becoming a very, very interesting story. But there is one author, whose name I have just forgotten, who compared the imploding "Russiagate" investigation with Russian wooden nesting dolls. He says this Russiagate story is like opening one doll, and there's another doll inside, and another inside that—but in the center there's absolutely nothing! This is now coming out, and it's backfiring.

Senator Chuck Grassley, and Senator Lindsey Graham, surprisingly enough, are now demanding that the FBI and the Department of Justice open a criminal investigation against Christopher Steele. There are many inconsistencies in what he has said in different locations. There is also a big demand now to get to the bottom of what happened to the 50,000 SMS text messages which miraculously were "lost." This is incredible: These were text messages exchanged between Peter Strzok from the FBI, and his FBI paramour, Lisa Page, covering the period between December 2016 and May 2017.

To lose 50,000 text messages, as former high-ranking NSA analyst William Binney points out, is virtually impossible, because the FBI and also the NSA had exactly the same records of the text messages, and to make them disappear simultaneously would not only require a willful action to erase it, but also, any hardware recording device would also have to be destroyed.

Senator Grassley has said that he will do everything in his power to somehow find a technical way to retrieve these missing texts. This is really like Watergate, where the cover-up was worse than the initial crime.

But from the texts that are already in the hands of the investigating committees in the Congress, it is now clear that Strzok and his paramour talked about a "secret society," which met repeatedly to plot to defeat the election campaign of Trump. After he did win the election, they plotted how to get him out of the White House.

Now, another senator, Ron Johnson (R-Minn.), says he has an independent informant who confirmed that "secret society" meetings to plot against Trump *did* take place, and this is all coming out now. As many Republican Congressmen have said, such corruption will lead not only to firing some of these people, but in all likelihood, to criminal charges.

Schlanger: Of course, we have to emphasize the British role in this, including circles around "former" British Intelligence officer Christopher Steele—this is beginning to emerge. What do you think the Congressmen should be looking at, in order to really get at the bottom of who initiated the plot and why?

Zepp-LaRouche: The initial reports came from British Intelligence, and the fact that Christopher Steele is supposedly a "former" MI6 agent, is also worth looking into. Because this dossier was probably outsourced to British intelligence, or to a cooperative effort between the Obama Administration and British intelligence. That is an area where some people have used the word "treason," and I think this is exactly what it amounts to. This is a bigger crime, in my view—bigger than Watergate, and probably the biggest criminal political action since the assassination of John F. Kennedy and its cover-up.

In any case, I think it is something which will not go away. There is no way that the questioning of Trump which Mueller is now trying to do, will derail the matter of the missing texts one bit.

Neocons Pushing Us to War

Schlanger: And I think the other side of the British question is in the dossier we provide on Mueller's history, showing that the initial investigation of your husband by the FBI was also initiated by British intelligence.

Now, the other issue is the leading British role in the escalation by the neocons for confrontation with Russia and China. We see that developing through a series of memos and discussion papers coming out. The Russians are responding very sharply, as are the Chinese now—so, catch us up on where that stands.

Zepp-LaRouche: The "Summary of the 2018 National Defense Strategy of the United States of America" was just issued, which calls Russia and China the worst security problem of the United States, worse than terrorism. It uses Cold War language. That has all kinds of implications. I find it quite interesting that some of the Chinese, and also Sergey Lavrov, the Russian Foreign Minister, reacted very, very strongly. I think we mentioned last week, that Lavrov made a very clear distinction between Trump's intention and what his opposition are trying to force him to do, because Trump is looking at the Senate where he can expect that all his vetoes on policy will be overridden.

It is quite noteworthy that the Chinese Ambassador to Washington, Cui Tiankai, just made a statement re-emphasizing that from China's standpoint, the relationship between the United States and China is one of "partners," and that this partnership is absolutely key to solving all the crucial problems in the world. So, I think it's really good that China is not responding in the same menacing language.

In a terrible contrast to that, there was a Federal press conference in Berlin, and the journalists asked the German government spokesperson, "What is the German attitude to this new U.S. defense paper?" And the spokesperson said, "Of course, for us, the United States is our most important ally, and we fully back up everything they do." It was totally outrageous, as if Germany had no interest in avoiding a conflict between the United States and Russia. It just shows you that Germany, at least as far as its official representatives are concerned, is still completely occupied—at least in the mind of the spokesperson. You could see the occupying forces clearly coming out of her mouth. It's terrible.

Schlanger: And even while we're seeing these kinds of security statements, defense documents, and so on coming out, President Trump is still insisting that he wants good relations with Russia and China.

Zepp-LaRouche: I think that Trump absolutely still intends to do what he promised in the election campaign, but he is surrounded by a lot of neocons in the Republican Party—and actually, the Democrats are really the

Nazi Azov Battalion in action in Ukraine, Feb. 25, 2017.

war party. They're obsessed with this Russiagate operation, and they're driving the confrontation continuously, so Trump is really having a very difficult time.

Schlanger: One of the leading areas of confrontation, which is developing in a very dangerous way, is Ukraine. What's going on there?

Zepp-LaRouche: Ukraine could easily become the number-one conflict and hot-spot on the planet. The Rada [parliament], which, as people probably remember, has a lot of Nazis sitting in it as parliamentarians, established a new law which effectively calls for retaking the Donbas, the pro-Russian part of eastern Ukraine, by military means, and by implication also taking Crimea. President Petro Poroshenko has not yet signed this bill, but they already have built up a military headquarters in order to prepare such a military action, and that could very, very clearly lead to a war between Russia and NATO. This is a very dangerous development, and it's outrageous.

There is now a report that AirTronic, a Texas-based military weapons firm, has delivered heavy weapons to Ukraine's nazi Azov Battalion. On the website of the Azov Battalion you can actually see that they're using the same grenade launchers which the United States gave them, and that U.S. military personnel are training them.

That same report also mentions that the Azov Battalion is training right-wing extremists from all over Europe, including in the use of heavy weapons, and in driving tanks. I remember that President Putin, quite a while ago, warned that if the Nazi coup in Ukraine were not neutralized, that there would be the danger of fas-

cism spreading all over Europe. If these right-wing military forces are being trained by the U.S.A., there must be an investigation. I remember that the U.S. Congress banned any arming of the Azov Battalion in 2015, and it would be very good if these congressmen would start to investigate this present outrage right away.

Schlanger: The same networks that helped to organize the neo-Nazi coup in Kiev, that overthrew a democratically elected President, are still very prominent. These are the same networks, the National Endowment for Democracy and others, that are behind the aggressive language being used against China and Russia.

Zepp-LaRouche: Yes, I think that we need to publish this, and people have to be aware that the war danger is *extremely* acute. I can only remind people again, of what former Secretary of Defense William Perry said in respect to the Hawai'i so-called "false alarm" of a ballistic missile attack. He pointed to the fact that we are only minutes away from thermonuclear Doomsday, because the nuclear weapons systems are on "launch on warning." A change of this policy is urgently required.

Schlanger: In contrast to this war talk, we're seeing interesting developments from Japan and also between North and South Korea. You mentioned this before, when we were talking before this broadcast. What's going on with Prime Minister Abe of Japan?

Zepp-LaRouche: This is one of the more enjoyable developments, because, as you know, Japan used to be closely allied with the United States, irrespective of

China President Xi Jinping (right) meets Japan Prime Minister Shinzo Abe in Da Nang, Vietnam, Nov. 11, 2017.

which President was in power. And while Abe is still a friend of Trump's—and he has said that repeatedly—he is also pointing out, again and again, how crucial it is to have cooperation between Japan and Russia. They're working very well together in the development of the contested Kuril Islands. That will be the basis for a long-awaited World War II peace treaty between Russia and Japan. Abe wants to conclude such a peace treaty while he is still in office, so that is in the foreseeable future.

Abe has also repeatedly emphasized that Japan is now cooperating fully with the Asian Infrastructure Investment Bank, founded by China, and with the Belt and Road Initiative of China. So here you have the case of a statesman who really changed for the better. He dropped a rather confrontational line towards China and Russia, while maintaining a good relationship with Trump. He was the first foreign leader to visit Trump after his election victory—but at the same time, he also emphasize the need to cooperate with Russia and China. I wish that some of the European leaders would follow in Abe's footsteps and take the same approach, because that would create a completely different dynamic. That also would help neutralize the warmongers in the United States. With the warmongers isolated, people would act

differently, rather than slavishly following whatever stupidity comes out of those circles that are pushing confrontation.

Time to Seize the New Opportunity

Schlanger: Abe also announced that he's going to go to South Korea for the Winter Olympics. What do you make of the developments of the last week between North and South Korea?

Zepp-LaRouche: That is actually also one of the better developments. Interestingly, it is not reported much by the mainstream media. The same media were very happy to report Korean developments when things were going badly. What happened is that the North Korean leader Kim Jong-un, in his New Year's address, had called on all the Korean people for a peaceful reunification of the two Koreas, and repeatedly said that they should not give in to challenges coming in the way of such an effort for reunification.

The North Korea delegation of Olympics planners and a group of musicians have arrived in Seoul. There is a big pop star from North Korea there, with her pop music orchestra, and they will play. They have created a joint women's ice hockey team, where North and South Korean women will play Olympic hockey together as one team. So I think this is all very good. And

Women's ice hockey team of North Korea arriving in Paji, South Korea, Jan. 25, 2018.

China Foreign Minister Wang Yi (right), Heraldo Munoz (center), Foreign Minister of Chili, and Hugo Martinez (left), Foreign Minister of El Salvador, at the Celac Forum Jan; 22, 2018.

after all, President Moon Jae-in of South Korea thanked Trump for his efforts which made this possible. He did not refer to the sometimes hawkish statements by Trump—but I think he was pointing to the fact that there were absolutely crucial back-channel discussions between the United States and North Korea, and also Russia and China and North Korea.

So this seems to be going in a good direction, and hopefully, given the fact that Abe will be there, this is one of the spots where dialogue is showing clear superiority to confrontation.

Schlanger: And in the background of this, you have the continuing momentum around the Belt and Road Initiative. I want to point out to our viewers that there was another article written about your intervention and your support for the Belt and Road, and your active involvement, that people can see on the Schiller Institute website. Otherwise, we have a report from CELAC, the Community of Latin American and Caribbean States, where a top Chinese official, Foreign Minister Wang Yi, was just there in Chile and Uruguay talking about the Belt and Road, to great acclaim from leaders there. What's happening with this?

Zepp-LaRouche: CELAC is now officially working with the Belt and Road Initiative of China, and this has boosted the mood in all of the Caribbean and Central American and South American countries, that there is a real perspective for doing exactly what Africa is doing.

You have two continents, which, in our past decades of efforts for a new world economic order, I always used to compare, namely Africa and Latin America. Because many years ago, when you looked at the map of these two continents, you would see absolutely no infrastructure. If there was a little bit of infrastructure, it would go from the port to the natural resources, and then stop dead at the place where the minerals or other resources were being exploited. That limited infrastructure was just for colonialist exploitation and never for the development of the interior of the continent, or commerce among nations. And this is now changing.

What China is now doing, both in Latin America, and in Africa, is realizing the kinds of development plans spoken of by Alexander von Humboldt in the Nineteenth Century, and by my husband Lyndon LaRouche over the past 40 years. He worked with José López Portillo in the beginning of the 1980s on exactly

Workers from China at a construction site for residential housing by CITIC Construction Co. Ltd. of China, in Venezuela.

such a development plan, which we called *Operation Juarez*. It was based on the idea that the entire Latin American continent should be integrated through infrastructure—where most countries speak Spanish, except that Brazil speaks Portuguese—but in a certain way this is much easier to integrate than the European continent, which has so many different nations and languages and cultures.

So what China is now doing is effectively the implementation of the kinds of plans which we had pushed at the beginning of the 1980s. This is a very good development: There are many countries such as Ecuador, Bolivia, and Chile, that are completely onboard. The Chinese model of economic transformation, of turning poor countries into countries where people have a future, and also a future orientation in advanced areas, like joint space exploration and space research—this is a very positive development. It is the leading dynamic in the world, and nothing will derail that, unless some people cause nuclear war. But short of nuclear war, I don't think anything will stop this.

Schlanger: And Helga, the Chinese can raise living standards, can raise 800 million people out of poverty in China, and now are doing the same thing in Africa and in South America—why can't we do that in Europe and the United States?

Zepp-LaRouche: In our last Schiller Institute conference, in Frankfurt, Nov. 25-26, we passed a resolution calling on the European nations to do what the Chinese are doing. China has now officially said—also mentioned by Liu He at the Davos conference—that China has only 30 million poor people left, while Europe has 90 million. Why can't Europe say, like China, that poverty is going to be eradicated by 2020? Obviously, for the United States, that should be done as well: Why should we live with a condition in which—I think in Germany, 45 individuals own as much wealth as half of the population; I think eight people in the world own as much as half of the world population. This is just totally crazy: Nobody can use that much money. It is just completely unjust and it should not be like that.

I think we have to have the commitment to have a decent living standard for all human beings on this planet. This is not just a question of justice, this is also the question of human potential which is being wasted when people are hungry. People are impeded from developing their creative potential when they are impoverished, and may have to hold down three jobs for their livelihood. We have to have the idea that we need a new paradigm of completely different thinking, given the human potential which can be developed once everybody has a decent living standard.

What is the meaning of life? Is it to eat five tons of caviar in your lifespan and have 20 Porsches and 5 yachts and 3 jets? Obviously not! Obviously, it is much more sensible to have a meaningful life, being a scientist, or an artist, or a good teacher. To have fulfillment in your life by contributing to the continued development of mankind as a whole, with whatever potential you have, in whatever share you can contribute.

We need a rethinking: this mindless thought that money controls the world, and that money is what makes you happy, has to be replaced by other ideas, like the Leibnizian idea of the pursuit of happiness, which is in the Declaration of Independence of the United States; and Leibniz did not mean making a lot of money. What Leibniz meant by happiness was the idea that the creative potential of each person has to be guaranteed and must be realized. And I think this is the New Paradigm being developed with the Belt and Road Initiative. Xi Jinping has said many, many times that this is not just "infrastructure," but that there is a cultural dimension to the Silk Road, and a space dimension to the Silk Road, and all this pertains to the creative potential of human beings. And I think people have to start discussing that!

We need to have a political discourse on what the future of humanity should be in 50 years, in 100 years from now. Do we not want to become adult, as a species, where people treasure other things than just material things? I think people should think about the fact that we are at the crossroads, where, if we do our job right now, and bring the United States and European nations into collaboration with the New Silk Road, then we can have a completely new era of civilization, probably in our lifetime. I appeal to our listeners, to you, to contact us, join us, help our efforts, and make what we are saying more known.

Schlanger: And as you've said so beautifully, that's what will make people happy, being able to do that. So, Helga, thank you for joining us, and we'll be back again next week.

Zepp-LaRouche: Yes, till next week.

The Memo Voted Out of Committee, McCabe Fired— First Steps To End the Coup?

by Barbara Boyd

Jan. 30—Monday night, Jan. 29, the House Select Committee on Intelligence voted to declassify a four-page memo authored by its staff, and called the "Nunes" memo by the news media, named after Committee Chairman Devin Nunes (R-Calif.). The memo will now go to President Trump, who has five days, under the Congressional declassification procedure used, to object to the memo's contents on national security grounds. Based on leaks to the press so far, the four-page memo includes the fact that a very dirty British intelligence product authored by MI6's Christopher Steele was used to initiate FISA surveillance of the Trump presidential campaign.

As was previously stated, some months back, by *EIR* in our dossier, "Robert Mueller Is an Amoral Assassin, He Will Do His Job If You Let Him," FBI and Justice Department officials dressed up the dirty British memo, and presented it to the FISA court without informing the court that the surveillance application (or applications) was based on a foreign intelligence source working directly for, and being paid by the Democratic National Committee and the Clinton Campaign. The FISA court also was not told that the claims of the Steele Memorandum, in the words of former FBI Director James Comey, were considered by the FBI to be "salacious and unverified." What else is in the four-page document has not been leaked to the press, but from the hysterical reactions, it is juicy.

Steele and the British conspired against Donald Trump with Obama's CIA chief John Brennan and other Obama intelligence personnel and officials, in addition

White House/Pete Souza

John Brennan.

FBI official Peter Strzok.

Press coverage pumping up Christopher Steele's dodgy dossier.

to the FBI. As *EIR* has continuously stressed, the reasons for the coup are located in the terror of the Anglo-American elites as the very decadent foundations of their post World War II "order" crumble. They know they are faced with an inevitable financial collapse. They believe that turning Russia and China into their satrapies represents potential salvation. Russia and

China are not cooperating, but instead are dedicating themselves to launching a new worldwide human Renaissance. Donald Trump, throughout his Presidential campaign, lambasted the Anglo-American neo-liberal globalists and their drive for World War, earning their eternal hatred.

The British intelligence Christopher Steele operation is the source of the fake and demonstrably absurd claim that Donald Trump was a Manchurian candidate blackmailed by Vladimir Putin, and that Putin, like some James Bond villain, used super-potent social media bots and computer hacks to brainwash the American population into voting for Donald Trump. This McCarthyite claim has been openly embraced by the Democratic Party, along with calls for state-sponsored media censorship, a new Cold War with Russia and China, violence against "deplorables" who voted for Trump, political assassination, independence from executive branch control or Congressional oversight for the FBI and intelligence agencies generally, and similar openly fascist tenets.

Also on Monday, Andrew McCabe, the Deputy Director of the FBI, was effectively fired by FBI Director Christopher Wray. McCabe's firing came after Wray viewed the Nunes memo in which McCabe's role in illegal activities against President Trump is apparently referenced, and after Wray was briefed on the preliminary findings of FBI Inspector General Michael Horowitz concerning his investigation of FBI handling of the Clinton email probe.

Wray had insisted, prior to viewing the Nunes memo and prior to a briefing on the Inspector General's preliminary findings, that he would not fire McCabe, but, instead, allow him to retire in March. It was the Horowitz investigation which unearthed the now infamous texts between former Clinton and Trump FBI case-agent Peter Strzok and his FBI mistress, Lisa Page. Those texts referred to an FBI "insurance policy" against Trump assuming the Presidency, an insur-

Xinhua/Yin Bogu

Deputy Director of the Federal Bureau of Investigation, Andrew McCabe, left, and Attorney General Jeff Sessions at the Justice Department, on July 13, 2017.

ance policy discussed in a meeting in McCabe's office.

The balance of these texts, during the critical time period following the election and up to the appointment of special prosecutor Mueller, were declared "missing" last week in a letter by the FBI to Congress, because of a "technical glitch." After the ensuing uproar, Inspector General Horowitz stepped forward and offered the information that he was recovering the texts using "forensic methods."

twitter

Andrew McCabe's wife Jill (left), received a huge contribution to her campaign for Virginia State Senate from Clinton money man and former Virginia Governor Terry McAuliffe (at right, with Hillary Clinton).

Andrew McCabe did not recuse himself from the Clinton investigation despite the fact that his wife received a huge campaign contribution from Clinton money man and general sleazeball, former Virginia Governor Terry McAuliffe. McCabe attended meetings at which his wife was recruited as a candidate by McAuliffe. These meetings occurred at a time when both McAuliffe and Clinton were under FBI investigation, and McCabe was the number two man in the FBI.

The money McAuliffe provided was to run a Virginia State Senate campaign against incumbent Senator Richard Black, and followed FBI harassment of Black for his very public condemnation of U.S. actions in Syria. McCabe was also photographed at his wife's campaign events, and Hillary Clinton herself came to Virginia to campaign for Jill McCabe, a State Senate candidate. This story has also been exclusively reported by *EIR*. But this clear conflict of interest and the President's appropriate anger about it, has been portrayed by the fake news media as inappropriate partisanship by Donald Trump, disrespect for the First Amendment rights of FBI agents and their spouses, and similar hysterical whole-cloth fabrications.

Late last week, as Congressional Republicans lined up to view the four-page Nunes memo and declared themselves "shocked" at the Constitutional abuses against President Trump that it revealed, Republican Senators Chuck Grassley and Lindsey Graham sent a letter to Democratic National Committee Chairman Tom Perez, other former DNC officials, and John Podesta, Hillary Clinton's campaign chair, seeking information about who in the DNC and Clinton Campaign knew about the Christopher Steele authored British intelligence dirty dossier and how it was utilized.

The letter seeks information about the shopping of the Steele dossier through both the Obama Administration and its intelligence agencies, and the national news media. Grassley and Graham, based on information available to them, classified or otherwise, had previously referred Christopher Steele to the United States Department of Justice for prosecution.

Of particular interest in the Grassley letter is a request for all communications of DNC and Clinton officials with former State Department official Jon Winer and former State Department operative Victoria Nuland.

House Select Committee on Intelligence Chairman Devin Nunes.

Nuland was the case officer for the 2014 United States-organized coup in Ukraine, which used neo-Nazis as its military front. Winer, a former counsel to John Kerry, is a U.S. friend of Christopher Steele and has vouched for him in U.S. government circles. Winer, otherwise, was deeply involved with British agent Bill Browder in securing the Magnitsky Act sanctions against Russia.

Does this mean that Grassley et al. have finally focused on the role of the British and U.S. State Department/Project Democracy elements central to the coup against Trump as well as the coup in Ukraine? If so, this is an investigative breakthrough.

The coup in Ukraine and the Magnitsky Act sanctions were deliberate geopolitical provocations by the Anglo-Americans against Russia, part of a general plan to isolate and debilitate Russia and China under conditions in which another Western economic collapse is a key strategic element. Christopher Steele had a previous relationship with the State Department concerning the Ukraine coup, issuing dozens of reports to Victoria Nuland and John Kerry. It is claimed that Steele's sources in the dirty Trump dossier were the same ones he sold to the State Department for the Ukraine coup.

The role of Ukrainian intelligence in the Clinton campaign and in the "Russia hacked the DNC" fabrication is of increasing interest to serious investigators. Ukrainian intelligence and associated State Department entities have played and are playing a leading role in imposing outright media censorship in the United States, based on false assertions that all dissenting voices here are controlled by the Russians.

C-SPAN

Senators Chuck Grassley (R-Iowa) and Lindsey Graham (R-S.C.).

Right: Ukraine coup case officer, former Assistant Secretary of State Victoria Nuland

Far right: Anti-Russian operative Bill Browder

CC/Mariusz Kubik

news-cycle binge of delusional denunciations about how reckless the House Intelligence Committee was and how the White House was coordinating a desperate drive to undercut Mueller and to obstruct justice. The President aptly described the situation in twitter fashion, "You fight back, it's obstruction."

It is reported that Mueller is fixated on claiming that Trump obstructed justice when he fired James Comey and when he allegedly said, in Comey's account, that he hoped the FBI would let the matter of Michael Flynn go. The corruption at the top of the FBI and the existence of an apparent "Get Trump" task force within Obama's intelligence community, makes Mueller's putative obstruction case, already constitutionally and legally outlandish, something akin to the fantasies of a dictator in a banana republic.

In Greek mythology, Hercules was given the task of cleaning the Augean stables of enormous amounts of cow dung which had accumulated from 3,000 cattle over thirty years. He had to do this in a single day. Hercules did so by diverting two rivers to accomplish the task. We have as little time to deal with what has accumulated at the FBI, the Department of Justice, and our other intelligence agencies under the auspices of the Bushes and the Obamas.

Additionally, the Grassley-Graham letter asks for any contacts between DNC officials and Cody Shearer. According to the Jan. 30 *Guardian,* Christopher Steele handed a copy of a memo written by Shearer to the FBI in October 2016, as "corroborative" of the outrageous claims made by Steele. Cody Shearer, according to press accounts, is a long-time dirty tricks operative on behalf of the Clintons.

In the wake of these events, the damage-control spinners in both the Republican and Democratic parties and in Robert Mueller's office, are on a desperate drive to salvage Robert Mueller's investigation and to salvage Russiagate. They are playing against time as the coup itself begins to unravel.

Ever since release of the Nunes memo was mooted, the media have been on a full

Xinhua/Ting Shen

Special Prosecutor Robert Mueller.

It was thirty years ago, that the prosecution of Lyndon LaRouche was being played out in a federal courtroom in Boston, with Robert Mueller, as U.S. Attorney, overseeing the show. It would be only fitting now, as a result of these events, if a river of public furor swept this country, ending the coup which is dividing and ruining us. The arc of the universe, after all, bends towards justice.

End the British War on America!

by Robert Ingraham

Jan. 27—The future of every American, as well as countless numbers of human beings worldwide, now depends upon the life-and-death political battle being waged inside the United States. That battle, however, has been completely misrepresented in the establishment news media, and is imperfectly understood even among many who are otherwise playing a positive role at this time.

On the one hand, various elements of the Democratic Party, remnants of the Obama Administration and the political attack-dogs of George Soros are all portrayed as constituting a partisan effort to remove Donald Trump from office, either through impeachment, the use of the 25th Amendment, or other means. Special Counsel Robert Mueller's ongoing witch-hunt sits in the center of these efforts. Many Democratic Party elected officials, out of either stupidity or fear, have fallen into this trap, with the role of the Black Congressional Caucus being perhaps the most tragic.

Concurrently, if one peruses almost any recent issue of an American newspaper, or watches a typical news program from CNN or other media outlets, the consumer of such "news" would be led to believe that there is now a powerful "neocon resurgence" within the United States, one which has attained hegemony—or near-hegemony—within the Trump Administration. The *New York Times,* for example, in its front page coverage of Trump's Dec. 18 speech, stated categorically that Trump's speech, and the accompa-

nying National Security report, signaled an extremely aggressive turn against both China and Russia, and it contrasted this new military aggressiveness with the more peaceful (!) policies of the previous Obama Administration.

Perhaps you have already taken a partisan position as to "where you stand" on these matters. If you watch MSNBC's Rachel Maddow you probably believe one thing; if your taste runs toward Sean Hannity, you believe another. But before you act, consider this: *you have been fooled.* Nothing described in the preceding two paragraphs is actually scientifically truthful. None of it represents an accurate picture as to what is going on in the world. So, before you start writing letters, making phone calls, or sending out tweets, consider the following.

Understanding Where We Are

As this is being written, the human species—and every nation on this planet—is at a moment not only of great, profound opportunity, but one where that opportunity is increasingly becoming reality. A new era for mankind is emerging within the spreading geometry of the global Belt and Road projects, including not only great economic projects, but entirely new axioms for relations among nations, axioms which are increasingly explicit, not merely implicit.

The win-win outlook, as put forward by Chinese President Xi Jinping, is rapidly becoming the international norm, as more and more nations are drawn into a policy of

Kremlin.ru

Russia President Vladimir Putin and President Donald Trump met at the G-20 summit in Hamburg, Germany, July 7, 2017.

Presidents Xi Jinping and Donald Trump, during the ceremony welcoming Trump to China, Nov. 9, 2017.

physical-economic development, great projects and peaceful cooperation. Rail, water, and electrification projects in Africa show what is possible, and the recent eager receptivity to this agenda at the China-CELAC conference of Carribean and Latin American nations is but one example of how the Belt and Road perspective is spreading world-wide (see article, page 20).

We are dealing here with long arcs of history, and in 2018 we are now nearing the end of one human era and the beginning of another. Since 1763, the British Empire, *including most emphatically its monetary and financial institutions,* has dominated world affairs. That empire has been challenged before, most notably by the American Revolution, by Abraham Lincoln, by Franklin Roosevelt, and others, but its hegemonic sway over human affairs has never been broken. That is now happening.

The implications of this are huge, and it is only possible to comprehend the current attacks and pressures on Donald Trump if one begins from that historic/global reality. The oligarchical power brokers of London are beyond desperation—this is their "Hitler in the bunker moment"—and they are lashing out.

Seeing through the Media Blather

All of the current anti-Trump operations emanate from London, and it is the British empire and the monarchy who are now engaged in a desperate effort to overthrow the government of the United States. A domestic "insurrection" against Donald Trump—be it from the left or right—as it is daily portrayed in the news media, does not exist. What we are witnessing is a foreign-directed assault on Constitutional government in the United States.

This British onslaught includes the wholly British-created and impeachment-intended "Russiagate" legal attacks on the Trump White House—attacks now exposed as originating entirely with MI6 operative Christopher Steele, the GCHQ, and other British entities. The onslaught also includes, however, the current effort by so-called "neocons" to wreck President Trump's positive foreign policy initiatives. These neocons—in both the Republican and Democratic parties, as well as in the U.S. national security establishment—far from being a "home grown" war faction, all march to the tune set by the London *Economist,* the Royal Institute for International Affairs (RIIA, Chatham House) and the RIIA's U.S. clone, the Council on Foreign Relations, along with the latter's many derivative and like-minded organizations. The war drive comes from London.

The entirety of the eight-year Obama Presidency was one not only of permanent war, where U.S. troops were officially engaged in combat for every single day of that administration's existence (the only Presidency in our history of which that is true), but also where a dramatic

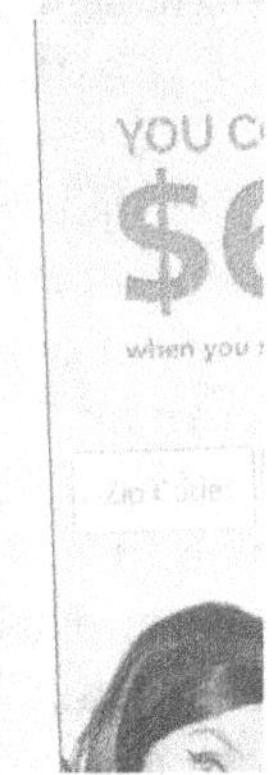

page from *Vanity Fair*

Example of the media blather to support the Mueller-led, anti-Trump coup attempt.

shift was implemented toward strategic war confrontation with both Russia and China. In reality, it is precisely the "interruption" of that war drive, occasioned by the fortunate victory of Donald Trump in the November 2016 election, that is motivating the British attacks on Trump today.

A Bit of Recent History

To comprehend the nature of today's battlefield, it is necessary to re-examine events which took place in the wake of the December 1991 dissolution of the Soviet Union. At that time, the proposals by Lyndon and Helga LaRouche for the establishment of a partnership with the new Russian state and for a "European Triangle" and "Eurasian Landbridge" economic development policy for the former Comecon nations, were rejected outright by the City of London and its allies in the George H.W. Bush Administration. Instead, it was agreed that Russia would be looted economically, dismembered, and extinguished as a strategic power. For the British throne this was to be the realization of its long-sought geopolitical goal to seize control of the Eurasian heartland, as spelled out decades ago by Sir Halford John Mackinder.

The George W. Bush Presidential Library

UK Prime Minister Tony Blair (left) at a meeting meeting with President George W. Bush in Crawford, Texas, in 2002. Blair was pressuring Bush to launch the war against Iraq.

Unfortunately for the British, the 1999-2000 accession of Vladimir Putin to power in Russia and the Putin-led victory in the Second Chechen War threw a monkey-wrench into their plans. At the same time, the economic and policy reforms initiated by Deng Xiaoping and carried through by his successors, culminating in the Belt and Road Initiative of current Chinese President Xi Jinping, have not only created the greatest economic miracle in modern history, but now anticipate a permanent end to the hegemony of British imperial trans-Atlantic rule.

To this day, most Americans remain oblivious to the true nature of British imperial policy. Even among honest patriotic American members of the military and the national security apparatus, there is an egregious error made in both misunderstanding British intentions, and denigrating the influence and power of British capabilities. Britain is viewed as the junior partner—with the emphasis on the word "junior"—in the "special relationship," and Britain's influence is often dismissed as insignificant.

Part of the reason that Britain's paramount role is denied, is a failure among many to comprehend the financial power that resides within the City of London, as well as in British control over many strategic raw materials. The modern British empire is a monetary empire, not a geographical one. Perhaps even more damaging is the whitewashing of historic British strategic designs. The real history of the last 200 years is largely unknown.

Throughout the 19th Century, the British Empire was considered the primary strategic and military adversary of the United States. Even up until the outbreak of World War II, Britain was viewed as an adversary, even a potential enemy—as seen in the official U.S. War Plans Orange and Red—with far different strategic interests than the United States.

It was only with the death of Franklin Roosevelt in 1945 that the grotesque "special relationship" would emerge. The two nations—which historically held antithetical political, economic, and strategic views—were now proclaimed to share a timeless cultural and political bond, with unified views on liberty, democracy and all aspects of policy. But it was not Britain which changed after 1945; it was the United States, a change which escalated dramatically following the 1963 murder of President John Kennedy.

America's Reichstag Fire

In a speech delivered on April 22, 1999 in Chicago, British Prime Minister Tony Blair unveiled a new Strategic Doctrine—to become known as the "Blair Doctrine"—in which he proclaimed an end to the Westphalian System of sovereign nation states, in favor of a new type of global interventionism, which he dubbed "a new type of war." As with all British utterances, Blair's words only revealed a portion of his intention. Explicitly, Blair was promulgating a doctrine of limited colonial war, but the actual targets were Vladimir Putin's Russia and the emerging economic power of China. This was an open proclamation announcing a new era of Anglo-American hegemonism globally, and this policy is precisely what Vladimir Putin denounced in his famous February 10, 2007 speech at the Munich Security Conference.

Twenty-nine months after Blair's speech, on Sept. 11, 2001, America was the target of the most heinous and murderous surprise attack since Pearl Harbor, an attack which ushered in the now-ongoing 17 years of permanent war. America was propelled into war in Iraq—with the aid of Tony Blair's lying "dodgy dossier"—with Britain and America acting in lockstep, as comrades in arms. During all of the subsequent military operations, Britain has played the role of our most steadfast "ally." The 9/11 attack was also the event which put the United States on a sustained semi-militarized footing, i.e., the creation of the "security state," with the FISA court, Homeland Security, and extensive surveillance of the American population, as revealed by Edward Snowden.

Sept. 11, 2001 attack on the World Trade Center in New York City.

From the beginning, the actual British authorship of the 9/11 attacks, particularly in collusion with and acting through their Saudi Arabian assets, was proven. This was documented in a Special Report published by *EIR*. It was our partner in the Special Relationship—our British "cousins"—who sent the planes into the World Trade Center. The intention of 9/11 was to force the shell-shocked United States into a policy of global permanent war, with the ultimate target being not Iraq or Afghanistan—but Russia and China.

Also, as documented by Barbara Boyd, it was none other than Robert Mueller—the current princeling of the Star Chamber that is targeting President Trump—who, as then FBI Director, classified the now notorious "28 pages" that provided proof of the Saudi role in 9/11, and it was Mueller who blocked Senator Bob Graham's investigation at every turn. Mueller intervened again and again to keep the truth about 9/11 from coming out.

As for Barack Obama, during his eight years in office, he exhibited complete fealty to the British Crown, and it was the British, once again, who led the way in overthrowing the government of Muammar Gaddafi in Libya in 2011, and then brutally torturing and murdering him.

Since 9/11, under Bush and even more so under

Robert Mueller, as FBI Director, blocked investigation of the Saudi role in 9/11.

President George W. Bush meeting with Saudi Arabian Ambassador Prince Bandar bin Sultan at the Bush Ranch in Crawford, Texas, Aug. 27, 2002.

White House/Pete Souza

President Barack Obama, offering a toast to Queen Elizabeth in London, May 25, 2011.

Obama, we have been living in a pre-war environment, something akin to Europe between 1905 and 1914. This is all British Empire geopolitics. In 1906, seasoned intelligence officer Col. William Robertson—later to be Field Marshal Sir William Robertson, Chief of the British Imperial General Staff—speaking on the growing threat to the British Empire from the rising economic might of Germany stated, "For centuries past we have thwarted ... each and every power in turn which has aspired to continental predominance; and concurrently, and as a consequence, we have enlivened our own sphere of imperial ascendancy. A new preponderance is now growing, of which the center of gravity is Berlin. Anything ... which would assist us in opposing this new and most formidable danger would be of value to us."

This is the evil British geopolitical outlook—one they mastered in the 19th Century—and this is how they view Russia and China today: enemies to be crushed.

Sarajevo

If 9/11 was the modern-day Reichstag Fire, the Sarajevo fuse which now threatens to unleash World War III was lit in 2014 in Ukraine. Between Feb. 18 and 26 of that year, the democratically-elected Ukrainian President Viktor Yanukovych was overthrown in a *coup d'état*—an illegal coup led by outright Nazis, and flagrantly backed and aided by the British government and the Obama Administration, including the personal role of Assistant Secretary of State for European and Eur-

asian Affairs Victoria Nuland.

Be clear! The Ukraine coup of 2014—and everything flowing from it during the last four years—poses a direct existential national security threat to the nation of Russia, including the potential full membership of Ukraine in NATO. During the last thirty-six months, the Russian response, led by President Putin, has been one of remarkable restraint, and this under conditions of escalating sanctions, economic warfare, and NATO expansion unleashed against Russia.

As a result of British and Obama policy, Russia is demonized today in ways that go beyond even the worst cold war propaganda. The day-in and day-out barrage of filth and lies that spews forth from the news media can have only one effect, which is to prepare the population for the inevitability of some type of military confrontation with Russia. Is it a bluff? A game of chicken? Only time will tell. But as the British have demonstrated repeatedly in the past, they are willing to go to war—even terrible genocidal war—to protect their geopolitical interests; and, as shown by the recent nuclear attack scare in Hawai'i, almost any provocation might set off the nuclear trigger.

China is also in the cross-hairs. Sanctions and other actions (such as requiring their news reporters to register as "foreign agents") are now being proposed against China, similar to what has already been done against Russia, and the same media whores who vomit hatred against Putin are now attacking the Belt and Road as a

U.S. Navy/Mass Comm. Spc. 2nd Class Julio Rivera

Marines embark in March 2011 for deployment to the Libyan coast.

cc/Mstyslav Chernov

Clashes in Kyev, the Ukraine capital, during the coup that overthrew President Viktor Yanukovych in February 2014.

strategic threat. It must be remembered that it was the British kiss-ass Obama's "Asia Pivot" which initiated a policy of military confrontation with China in East Asia.

The Assault on Donald Trump

Sixteen months after the British/Obama coup in Ukraine, on June 16, 2015, Donald Trump announced his candidacy for the Presidency. During that campaign he stated repeatedly, on the record, that he was irrevocably committed to ending the sixteen-year policy of regime change and permanent war. He spoke often of his desire to rebuild relations with Russia. And he vowed to rebuild the infrastructure and industry of America.

As has now been revealed in documents that have come to light, the targeting of the Trump candidacy by the FBI and other agencies began long before the election, even as early as 2015 when his chances were being dismissed by every political expert. From the start, the impetus for the attacks against Trump, as well as lying libelous written reports, originated with Christopher Steele and other British spook sources. And after the election, even as the get-Trump apparatus went into high gear, it was the lame duck Barack Obama, who during November 2016-January 2017, escalated provocations against Russia, including new sanctions, to poison the well for the incoming Trump Administration.

Let us speak plainly. Everything we are seeing today—in regard to the attacks and pressures on Trump—stems from a concerted foreign attack on Constitutional government in the United States. Since November 2016, the primary strategic goal of the British empire has been to overturn the results of that election, destroy Trump, and return the United States to the policy axioms of the Obama Administration. We are now in a full-blown foreign-led insurrection against the President of the United States, a British effort to overthrow the U.S. government. There are various components of this attack, but it is all one unified operation.

It is the British who are pushing a war policy. Open your eyes and take in the full picture. Pick up a copy of the London *Economist* and read one of its editorials. The British are terrified that a United States, under Trump, might escape from their geopolitical grasp. And then they will be alone.

Whether it is Robert Mueller, elements of the FBI, elements of the National Security apparatus, or deluded members of Congress—the individuals now involved in the treasonous insurrection are all *de facto* foreign agents, acting to overturn the election and return the United States to full strategic partnership with Britain, as existed under Obama, to revive and unleash a war drive, under British direction.

Victory

Ask yourself: Where in history, where in the universe are you? What is the nature of the opportunity which now exists?

There is no reason to get caught in limited pragmatic thinking or stupid political tactics. There is no cause for pessimism. Far from it. China's Belt and Road initiative is transforming the world and bringing the fifty-year mission of Lyndon LaRouche to fruition. Damocles' sword hangs by a thread over the British imperial financial system, ready to drop at any moment. A new era is now already being built.

Meanwhile, Robert Mueller's Russiagate investigation has been seriously damaged, perhaps fatally, and the alleged "resurgence of the neocons" has yet to be demonstrated as anything other than wishful thinking by the British crowd. President Trump's visit to Beijing last November shows what is possible. Our job—those who are associated with the historic mission of Lyndon LaRouche—is to identify and defeat this British attack on our nation and to bring America into the win-win future of global cooperation and economic development that is beckoning. This is our fight to win.

China-Celac Forum Embraces China's Belt and Road: Will the U.S.A. Join?

by Cynthia R. Rush

Jan. 29—In a dramatic development that would have seemed impossible just eight months ago, on Jan. 22 the 33 member-nations of the Community of Latin American and Caribbean States (Celac), a region encompassing all of the Western Hemisphere minus Canada and the United States, officially endorsed China's Belt and Road Initiative (BRI)—now the world's dominant development perspective. Meeting in Santiago, Chile under the title, "Working for More Development, Innovation and Cooperation for our People: A Common Destiny," the Second Ministerial Meeting of the China-Celac Forum, which included China's Foreign Minister

Wang Yi and his delegation, issued a formal declaration supporting the BRI, and expressing its desire to be an active participant in this magnificent development program.

Although the text of that statement is not yet available to *EIR*, Wang Yi's remarks to the China-Celac Economic and Trade Cooperation and Business Forum, which met one day later, left no doubt of Celac's commitment:

During the [Ministerial] meeting, the Foreign Ministers issued a special declaration on sup-

Xinhua/Xu Rui

China Foreign Minister Wang Yi, reading a congratulatory letter from President Xi Jinping during the second ministerial meeting of the China-Celac Forum in Santiago, Chile, Jan. 22, 2018.

porting and participating in the Belt and Road Initiative. It means that with the Second Ministerial Meeting, *this visionary Initiative put forward by [China's] President Xi Jinping has been extended to Latin America and the Caribbean, and become the largest and most welcomed platform for international cooperation spanning all continents and oceans.* It is also the most important public goods that China provides to the world.

China and Celac agreed to jointly build the Belt and Road. As China and other countries work together on the Belt and Road Initiative, LAC [Latin American and Caribbean] countries cannot be absent and should be a meaningful part of it. The ancient Maritime Road had once connected us across the Pacific Ocean. Now, in the 21st Century, China stands ready to work with the LAC countries to revitalize it. Collaboration in this process will create greater space and markets, as well as resources and means for the development of LAC countries.

In his congratulatory letter to the Jan. 22 Ministerial meeting, read by Wang Yi, Xi Jinping underscored:

Historically, our ancestors, braving the waves of the vast ocean, blazed the trans-Pacific Maritime Silk Road between China and the LAC countries. Today, we need to draw a new blueprint for our joint effort under the Belt and Road Initiative, and open a path of cooperation across the Pacific Ocean that will better connect the richly-endowed lands of China and Latin America.... Let us join hands and set sail toward a better future for China-LAC relations and for humankind.

The China-Celac Forum

The China-Celac Forum was founded in July 2014, during the annual summit of the BRICS nations

Xinhua/Xu Rui

Chinese Foreign Minister Wang Yi (front R) attends a meeting with foreign ministers from Chile, the Dominican Republic, Ecuador and Haiti, as well as the representative of El Salvador, in Santiago, Chile, Jan. 21, 2018.

(Brazil, Russia, India, China, and South Africa), held that year in Fortaleza, Brazil. During that summit, President Xi Jinping met separately with all the leaders of Celac, including eleven heads of state. At the First Ministerial Meeting in Beijing the following January, the China-Celac Forum presented a 2015-2019 Action Plan based on the framework of a "1+3+6" formula: "one plan" (the 2015-2019 Action Plan), "three motors" (trade, investment and finances), and "six fields," (energy, infrastructure building, agriculture, manufacturing, technological innovation and information technology).

There was great optimism coming out of that first Beijing meeting, reflected also in the simultaneous forward motion of the BRICS nations. But by the end of 2015 and going into 2016, this optimism was tempered by a series of *de facto* coups d'état in the region, which installed governments friendly to Wall Street and hostile to the BRICS and the BRI. Neoliberal Mauricio Macri won Argentina's presidency in December 2015; in May 2016, President Dilma Rousseff of BRICS member Brazil was illegally ousted in a bankers' coup and replaced by the monetarist Michel Temer; and Wall Street banker Pedro Pablo Kuczynski, or PPK, became Peru's President in July that year.

All three have wreaked economic and political havoc in their respective countries, while claiming to favor cooperation with China, and seeking Chinese investments in some key areas. Ideologically, however, they are wedded to the old paradigm of British geopoli-

Chilean President Michelle Bachelet (left) meeting China Foreign Minister Want Yi in Santiago, Chile, Jan. 22, 2018.

tics. Yet, the breathtaking speed with which the entire region has moved into the China-inspired New Paradigm over the past 7-8 months, threatens to make them all irrelevant. London and Wall Street, meanwhile, are still trying to figure out how this sea change happened right under their noses.

Having traveled to the LAC region three times since he announced the BRI in November 2013, visiting a total of ten countries, Xi Jinping wasn't deterred by events on the ground. At the May 2017 Beijing Belt and Road Forum on International Cooperation, there was no mistaking his message: "Latin America is the natural extension of the new 21st Century Maritime Silk Road." Eight months later, the region is brimming with enthsiastic debate about its future as part of the Belt and Road Initiative.

Chile's outgoing President, Michelle Bachelet, a staunch ally of China and firm supporter of the BRI, summed the situation up nicely in a Nov. 23, 2017 speech in Santiago celebrating the tenth anniversary of the Confucius Institute at the Santo Tomás University. Today, she said, the world is orienting "more than ever" toward China and the Pacific Basin, and therefore, "we know very well that our relationship with China and the Asia-Pacific … is crucial for us to fulfill our destiny." China's relationship with Chile goes well beyond trade ties, she added. "It is one of our primary *political* partners on the path to openess, integration and cooperation for progress."

Whither the United States?

In the course of the one-day summit Jan. 22, Wang Yi, as well as other speakers, described the current global strategic situation as fraught with "many uncertainties … and complexities." In that context, however, Wang Yi emphasized that China is a totally "reliable partner" whose foreign policy is based on "win-win" collaboration, mutual respect, a commitment to multilateralism, and non-intervention in other nations' internal affairs, seeking only to "share its development dividends with all other countries and achieve common prosperity." This, he said, reflects the "new kind of international relations" outlined by the recent 19th Congress of China's Communist Party.

He pointedly stated that China "has the resolve and confidence to explore a way of building a great country, *that is different from the one followed by the traditional powers,* and will always stand side by side with the LAC countries and all other developing countries." Geopolitical contest "or zero-sum game is neither our purpose nor our practice," he underscored. "We invite all countries, big and small, to discuss the BRI as equals."

None of the speeches at either of the Santiago meetings ever mentioned the United States explicitly. But implicit in the debate and intense diplomacy that took place over two days, was the obvious question of where the United States stands in this rapidly changing situation. Will the Trump Administration join China in the BRI's magnificent regional—and global—development perspective? Or will it exclude itself as desired by the British-linked elements which are attempting to overthrow the U.S. Presidency? These latter elements want to claim that China's growing presence south of the border constitutes "aggression" against U.S. interests in its traditional "backyard."

The rapid turn of events in the region has already set off alarm bells among the proponents of British geopolitics in Washington. Last December the National Endowment for Democracy (NED)—a key instrument of regime-change and "color revolutions" carried out internationally over the last several years in the name of "democracy"—issued a panicked report entitled "Sharp Power, Authoritarian Influence," decrying China's growing presence in the LAC region. Its chief complaint is that with its economic achievements, impressive growth, and growing global influence, China can now offer the prospect "of economic opportunities" to the LAC region that other international partners cannot match.

The NED specifically targets the China-Celac Forum as the purveyor of China's allegedly nefarious influence, charging that through its ministerial and related meetings, Beijing "can leverage more agenda-setting power with regard to the region" than it has been able to achieve by more traditional means. Worriedly, it warns of the great danger that an increasing number of the region's political elites, students, scientists, cultural representitives and other "renowned influential people," are coming under Beijing's "hypnotic" spell, after traveling to China on all-expenses-paid trips, and then returning home as "*de facto* ambassadors of the Chinese cause"!

Build the World Land-Bridge

In contrast to this claptrap, in a Jan. 17 discussion, Schiller Institutes founder Helga Zepp-LaRouche outlined a sane path for the United States to follow, noting that it is only by bringing real economic development to Central America and the Caribbean, in particular—regions suffering from often horrific economic conditions and corresponding human suffering—that the United States can begin to effectively address such acute domestic problems as the drug epidemic or immigration. U.S. collaboration with China in the region would allow for the building of large infrastructure projects—ports, railways, new industries, and transportation corridors—by which the region could progress quickly, reaching higher levels of productivity and putting its people to work.

The United States itself is in urgent need of large investments in infrastructure and high-technology projects, and China has offered to partner with it in building them. If built on the necessary scale with the most advanced technologies, including high-speed rail lines, transportation corridors and new cities, construction of these projects would ensure the extension of the World Land-Bridge through all of North America, and across the Bering Strait into Eurasia. It would also be of great benefit to the United States to have a thriving, economically developing Caribbean and Central American region on its southern border.

Xinhua/Dan Hang

Panama President Juan Carlos Varela (L) and China Foreign Minister Wang Yi inaugurate China's embassy in Panama City, Panama, Sept. 17, 2017.

China intends to move forward in the region, but would much prefer to have the United States as a partner. "Join us," was the message delivered by Wu Changsheng, director of the Latin American Studies Center at the China Foundation for International Studies, in remarks to *Global Times* published Jan. 18. "China's cooperation with Latin American and Caribbean countries is not exclusive," he said. "It's inclusive. We welcome the participation from a third party. So the United States doesn't need to worry."

The Panama Case

This was the point Panama's President Juan Carlos Varela also made last June, shortly after Panama announced it had broken diplomatic ties with Taiwan and established them instead with the Peoples' Republic of China (PRC). Panama considers the United States a strategic partner, Varela said, and sees no contradiction in maintaining diplomatic ties with both powers. Washington should not view this as a threat to its interests, he correctly emphasized.

Panama's transformation since last June has been stunning, in order, as the Panamanians explain it, "to make up for lost time." Varela made a state visit and week-long tour of China last November, and Xi Jinping has accepted his invitation to visit Panama on a soon-to-be-announced date. There is a constant flow of diplomatic and technical delegations going back and forth between the two nations, and intense discussion of expanding economic, trade, and cultural ties. High on the agenda of priority development projects is the strategically important high-speed rail line extending from Panama City north to the border with Costa Rica. The pre-feasibility study for this, to be conducted by Chinese firms, will get underway very soon.

The project involves building two sets of double-tracked rail lines—one for passengers which will go as far as the city of David, and the other for freight, which will extend another 50 km to Paso Canoas in Chiriqui Province on the Costa Rican border.

China clearly intends the train to extend through Costa Rica and the rest of Central America to Mexico, for the purpose of vastly increasing regional cargo shipping to and from China, whose ships through the Panama Canal reportedly now return only 40% full. This sharp increase in regional trade will require expanding both the Panama City and Colón ports, at either end of the Canal, along with airports and other major infrastructure. China Airlines is already negotiating direct flights to Panama from Guangzhou, Shenzhen, and Shanghai, to begin in March of this year.

The implications of these plans have sparked enthusiastic debate in neighboring Costa Rica, the only other Central American nation to have diplomatic relations with the People's Republic of China. In a Dec. 19, 2017 article published in the Costa Rican daily *La Nación*, entitled "Panama Challenges Costa Rica," former Planning Minister Carlos Manuel Echeverría pointed out that Panama, "with its Canal and location, is already part of this [New Silk Road], and the challenge it has posed to Central America, without saying so, but which is self-evident, is that of continuing that railroad up to Mexico. Otherwise the one that is planned [inside Panama] will only be marginally useful."

Echeverría recalled that plans for such a rail line existed as far back as the 1980s, and even earlier, to promote regional integration. Today, he asked, "Why should we remain outside the Silk Road? It would be a crass mistake not to think strategically" and be left out of this exciting development. He observed that over just a few years, Panama has made huge advances, with an expanded Canal, a new large airport and subway system, and major infrastructure construction. So now, Echeverría concluded, it's time for Costa Rica to be bold, "to radically change its way of thinking, organize itself and act," starting with "thinking big."

A Diplomatic Anachronism

That boldness has so far not extended to the four Central American nations which the train would have to traverse (Nicaragua, El Salvador, Honduras and Guatemala), but whose governments still maintain diplomatic ties with Taiwan. The train would not go through Belize, the fifth Central American nation which continues to maintain ties with Taiwan. In the Caribbean, the Dominican Republic, Haiti, Saint Lucia, Saint Kitts and Nevis, and Saint Vincent and the Grenadines maintain ties with Taiwan as well.

But given the rapid changes of the past several months, particularly in Panama, this diplomatic anachronism may not last much longer.

Despite the lack of formal diplomatic ties, China has maintained consistent economic, trade, and cultural relations with all these countries, the most striking example of which is the proposed $4.7 billion project to rebuild the Haitian capital of Port-au-Prince. At the China-Celac Forum, the foreign ministers of these "holdout" nations nonetheless engaged in lively discussion with Wang Yi and his delegation. El Salvador's Foreign Minister Hugo Martínez, who is Celac's President Pro Tem, was visibly enthusiastic at the prospect of participating in the BRI. Wang undoubtedly made clear, as Wu Weihua, the Chargé d'Affaires at China's Panama embassy, did last August, that "China intends to replicate the Panama example in other countries in the region," including offering "juicy" investments of the kind Panama is now enjoying.

The Challenges Ahead

The 2019-2021 Action Plan agreed to by the China-Celac Forum is extremely ambitious and poses several challenges to the region, the most pressing of which is to accelerate movement away from its traditional role as a raw-materials exporter, toward industrialization and infrastructure development. This is a top priority for the region's governments.

Of the five major points of the new Action Plan which Wang Yi presented on Jan. 22, one calls for "developing competitive and sovereign home-grown industries," based on the most advanced technologies. "China has the equipment, technology, funding and training opportunities you need," Wang told his audience. "Our two sides may speed up industrial cooperation, work to build logistics ... broaden financing channels ... explore the establishment of a consortium of development-financial institutions, and build more in-

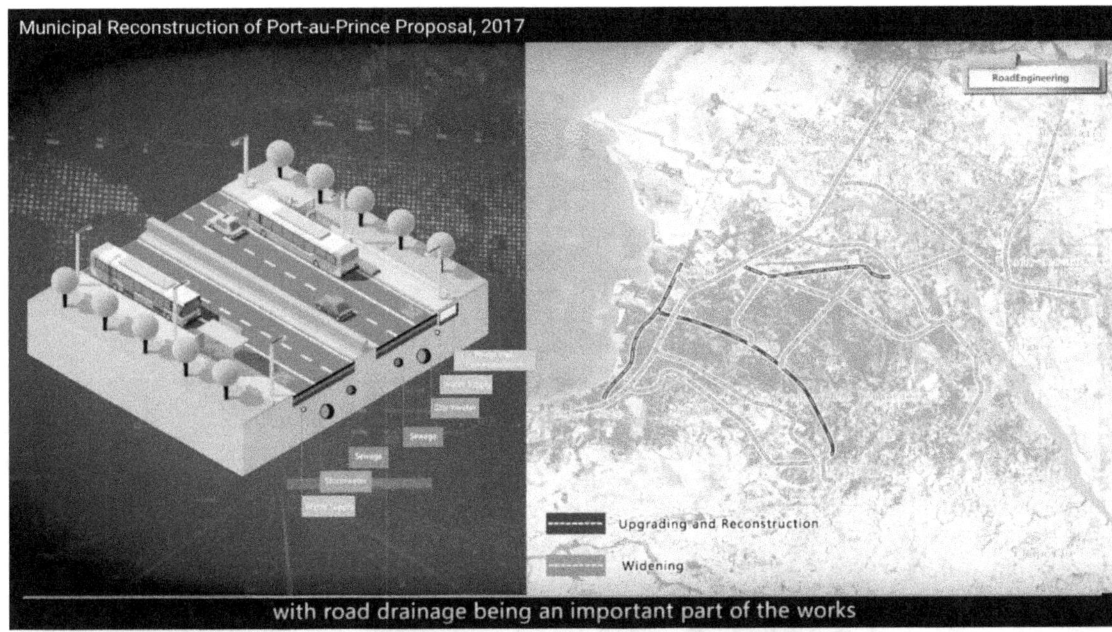

$4.7 billion plan by China to renovate the Haitian capital, Port au Prince, was accepted by Mayor Ralph Youri Chevy, Aug. 25, 2017.

Graphics from China's Southwest Municipal Engineering Design and Research Institute (SMEDRIC) video illustrating its Port-au-Prince project.

dustrial parks and special economic zones."

Wang also stressed the Action Plan's determination to "seize the opportunity of innovation-driven growth, enhancing coordination between the Belt and Road's Science, Technology, and Innovation Cooperation Action Plan, and the development strategies of LAC countries." This will involve building a China-LAC Silk Road and a digital Silk Road. This point calls for advancing "cooperation in emerging areas, such as aerospace and aviation ... China is ready to help train more researchers from LAC countries through the China-LAC Science and Technology Partnership and the China-LAC Young Scientists Exchange Program."

Of great importance is the Plan's proposal to build a transportation network connecting lands and oceans, emphasizing China's support "for building the bi-oceanic railways and tunnels, and open more sea routes and direct air links."

Another key component of the Action Plan is the commitment to intensify cultural and "people-to-people" exchanges. China, Wang said, "is ready to share more governance experience with LAC countries, enhance ... exchanges between our political parties" and other national organizations involving media, youth, and scientific groups, as well as establishing more cultural centers "and more Confucius Institutes in LAC countries to deepen mutual understanding and friendship."

No one doubts that implementing the Action Plan will require hard work and very close collaboration. But as Wang Yi stated at the end of his presentation, "As a Chinese poem reads, 'True friends value their promises to each other and will travel a thousand miles to be together.' Let us make this meeting a new starting point in our relations, seize the opportunity offered by the Belt and Road Initiative, and join hands across the ocean to open a splendid new era of China-LAC relations."

Davos: China's Belt and Road Stole the Show

by Mike Billington

Jan. 29—Events at the 48th annual World Economic Forum (WEF) in Davos, Switzerland this year, reflected the fact that the focus of world attention is now on China and its world-historic Belt and Road Initiative (BRI). Even the official theme of the Forum, "Creating a Shared Future in a Fractured World," came directly from the speech presented by Chinese President Xi Jinping at the 2017 Davos Forum, where he said: "Today, mankind has become a close-knit community of shared future," and declared his commitment to "the goal of building a community of shared future for mankind."

Professor Klaus Schwab, who founded the Davos WEF in 1971, and still serves as its Executive Chairman today, introduced Liu He, the keynote speaker from China to this year's Forum, who is also the leading economist in the transformation taking place in China today. In that introduction, Prof. Schwab said:

"Our community will recall the historic speech of President Xi Jinping at last year's Forum, which many participants felt was a turning point in China's relationship with the world. During the year, other important meetings took place, like the Belt and Road Forum, the G-20, and APEC, in which President Xi continued to further develop many points that he raised in his Davos speech, leading to the 19th Party Congress speech, in which he outlined his great vision for China's new era."

Professor Schwab also noted that China was "simultaneously shifting the current mix of industrial sectors, while at the same time investing in the development of

World Economic Forum/Sandra Blaser

Liu He (left), member of ruling Central Committee and Director of the General Office for the Central Leading Group for Financial and Economic Affairs, and Klaus Schwab, Founder and Executive Chairman of the World Economic Forum, speaking during the session "China's Economic Policy," at the 2018 annual meeting of the forum in Davos, Switzerland, Jan. 24, 2018.

new technologies, to become the *leader* in new technologies, and the creation of future industries in order to leapfrog ahead."

The character of the entire Davos Forum this year was captured by the *New York Times* reporter attending the event, Keith Bradsher. In an article in the *Times* on Jan. 28 under the title, "At Davos, the Real Star May Have Been China, Not Trump," Bradsher bemoaned the fact that, like it or not, it was China's New Silk Road that dominated the Forum, not the efforts by many to demean the Belt and Road Initiative as merely China's effort to "spread its influence" and to "bury the recipients in debt and cause considerable environmental damage," as Bradsher also reported.

Under a picture of a smiling Liu He making his keynote presentation, Bradsher acknowledged that Liu

White House/Shealah Craighead

President Donald Trump greeting British Prime Minister Theresa May upon her Jan. 27, 2017 arrival at the White House.

He's presentation was "one of the best-attended speeches," and that throughout the Forum, the Belt and Road was the leading subject of discussion. "At one end of town, President Michel Temer of Brazil welcomed an unexpected offer from Beijing for Latin American nations to work closely with a Chinese initiative," writes Bradsher. "At the other end of town…, Pakistan's Prime Minister Shahid Khaqan Abbasi used his talk to praise the rapidly expanding Chinese investments in his country, including to build power stations and a large port."

Bradsher concluded: "National leaders seemed to vie with one another in Davos in calling for closer cooperation with China." He quoted Joe Kaeser, the chief executive at Siemens: "The China One Belt, One Road is going to be the new WTO—like it or not."

Bradsher also noted that China was simultaneously mobilizing development projects around the world: "On Friday, the Chinese government used a policy document issued in Beijing to call for a Polar Silk Road that would link China to Europe and the Atlantic via a shipping route past the melting Arctic ice cap … at a summit meeting for Latin American and Caribbean foreign ministers in Santiago, Chile, Foreign Minister Wang Yi of China called for close cooperation and participation by the region's countries."

Liu He

The keynote by Liu He focused primarily on the policies which have made possible the transformation of China into a primary driving force—perhaps *the* primary driving force—in world growth and technological innovation, and the importance of the Belt and Road Initiative. But he also issued a warning about the risk of a global crisis: "At such a critical moment we must focus on the spillovers of the monetary policy of the world's major economies, and changes in the debt, equity, and commodity markets in the short term. In the medium term we need to pay attention to the question of labor productivity and to the changing savings rates in the large economies…. Meanwhile, deep-seated problems in the world economy have yet to be fixed. Multiple risks and considerable uncertainties come in the form of high debt, asset bubbles, protectionism, and the escalation of global and regional hot-spots. To turn cyclical recovery into sustainable growth, we need concerted global efforts."

We hope that President Trump has the opportunity to read the seminal work by Liu He in his study of the 1930s Great Depression and the more recent 2007-8 financial crash. In that study, completed in 2013, Liu noted the disastrous consequences of failing to distinguish between the "real economy" and the "fictitious economy." Liu He wrote:

"We should avoid moving to an over-indebted economy, and attach importance to regulating and controlling financial fluctuations. We must uphold the essential requirements of financial services for the real economy. The departure of the U.S. financial industry from its core service function has become the perpetrator of the global financial crisis. This is related to the abandonment of the traditional value of the industry by the U.S. financial industry and excessive pursuit of wealth and innovation [referring here to innovation in speculative instruments by the major banks and hedge funds—ed]. Various effective measures should be taken to both improve the business environment of the real economy, consolidate the foundation for the development of the real economy, and to curb capital from empty money-making-money schemes so as to prevent excess self-circulation and inflation in the fictitious economy."

The ballooning of the U.S. stock market is primarily due to such "schemes," rather than to actual economic growth.

China Offers New Silk Road To Northern Europe Through the Arctic Back Door

by Ulf Sandmark

Ulf Sandmark writes from Sweden.

Jan. 20—Thousands of regular cargo trains of the Chinese Belt and Road Initiative (BRI), or the New Silk Road (NSR), have reached Western Europe. But in Northern Europe the cargo trains only reach as far as the shores of the Baltic states (the harbors of Riga in Latvia, and Klaipeda in Lithuania) and the railway station at Kouvola in Eastern Finland. Now, however, China is reaching out to the coasts of Scandinavia and Northern Europe through the Arctic "back door" from the Pacific Ocean, using the Northern Sea Route (NSR), which stretches its way westwards to Europe between the polar ice and the northern Siberian coast.

Actually, Hu Angang, a leading Chinese economist at Tsinghua University, coined the term "One Circle"—referring to the encirclement of the entire Eurasian land mass by the completion of the northeast passage—to go along with the "One Belt, One Road." The ongoing melting of the Arctic ice—a phenomenon of the far North not to be confused with non- existent global warming—makes this sea route practicable already today. Russia is building a series of the world's largest icebreakers in order to expand the use of this route. China officially included the Arctic Route as part of the Maritime Silk Road in its "Vision for Maritime Cooperation under the Belt and Road Initiative" of June 20, 2017.

Just days ago on January 26, the Chinese government launched its first Arctic Policy White Paper towards building a "Polar Silk Road." The policy paper says that China hopes to work with all parties to build a "Polar Silk Road" by developing the Arctic shipping routes. Chinese enterprises are encouraged to participate in infrastructure development for these routes and

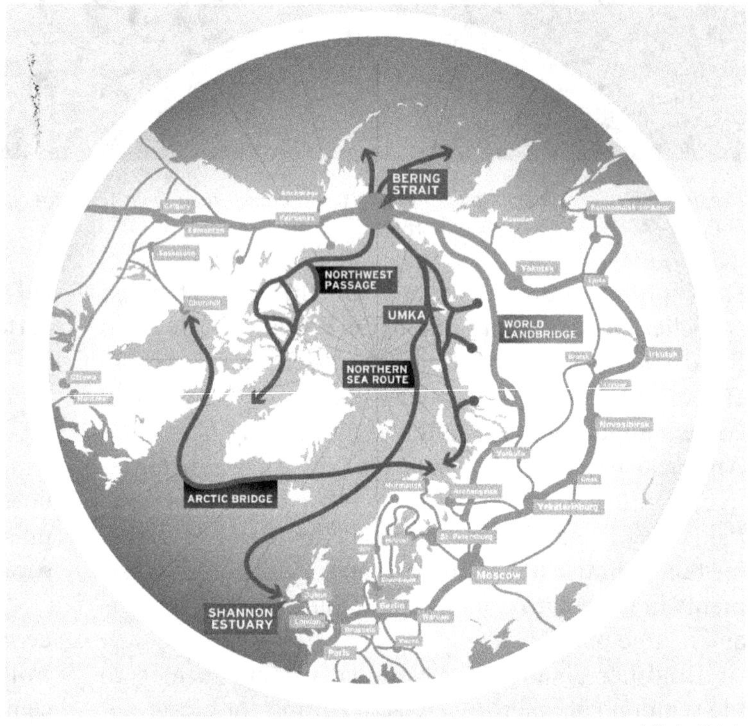

schillerinstitut.de

View of Arctic polar land and sea routes.

conduct commercial trial voyages. China is also eyeing development of oil, gas, mineral resources, fishing and tourism in the region, jointly with the Arctic States, while respecting the traditions and cultures of the Arctic residents including the indigenous peoples, and conserving the natural environment.

The resources waiting to be developed—waiting only for the human race to discover the technologies needed to facilitate such development in a harsh environment, in a manner acceptable to human habitation—include vast deposits of gold and other minerals, as well as an estimated 30% of the world's undiscovered natural gas and 13% of its undiscovered oil, according to the U.S. Geological Survey.

The Independent
Barents **Observer**

LNG carrier "Christophe de Margerie" at port in Sabetta. Photo: Yamal Nenets

New era starts on Northern Sea Route

Today's shipment of LNG from Sabetta marks the onset of a period of big growth in Russian Arctic shipping.

Yamal Nenets

The new harbor of Sabetta and Russia's new Northern Latitude Railway open up the exploitation of the huge gas fields by the Arctic Yamal LNG project.

Along the NSR, the huge gas fields on Siberia's Yamal Peninsula are just now being opened up. It is about two thirds of the way from the Pacific to the Atlantic at the northern end of the Ural Mountains. The huge natural gas deposits of this region are being developed by a consortium involving Russia's Novatek, France's Total, and the China National Petroleum Corporation. Japan is also involved. There at the mouth of the Ob River, the brand-new big harbor of Sabetta has been built along with Russia's Arctic flagship project, the Yamal LNG project. The new Northern Latitude Railway connects Yamal with the Russian railway system to the south, ensuring year-round transport of the region's mineral resources.

At the same time, the world's largest liquefied natural gas (LNG) tanker, *Christophe de Margerie,* has been built by Daewoo Shipbuilding Marine Engineering (DSME) in Korea. Just weeks ago on December 6, 2017, it set out on its first trip from Sabetta. This tanker carries up to 172,600 cubic meters of LNG, has ice-protec-

tion level Arc7, and is capable on its own of breaking through 2.1 meters of ice. It is the first of 15 ships of this kind to serve the new natural gas project. The tanker has an engine power of 45 MW, which is "comparable to a nuclear-powered icebreaker," natural gas company Novatek says.

Even by itself, the Yamal LNG project will result in a major growth in Russian Arctic shipping, as it alone will produce up to 17 million tons per year. A second projected LNG plant, Arctic LNG-2, will produce another 17 million tons when it comes online, presumably in 2023. The estimates from the Russian Ministry of Natural Resources show that shipping volumes could increase to as much as 67 million tons by 2025 and to 72 million tons in 2030. Half of it will be LNG, and much of it will be shipped eastwards into Asia through the ice-covered waters of the Russian east Arctic, the *Independent Barents Observer* reports.

Initially, the shipments along the NSR will primarily involve its eastern part, servicing the Yamal project, and also deliveries of heavy machinery up the river Ob-Irtysh. On its maiden voyage in August 2017, the tanker *Christophe de Margerie* traveled from the LNG plant at Melkoya at the Northern tip of Norway, to South Korea in 19 days. It was a record time—actually only six days, 12 hours and 15 minutes for the NSR part, and also the

cc/Kabelleger

A LORE class pair of electric locomotives built in Germany, belonging to the Swedish MTAB company—designed to pull ore trains—is shown here pulling empty ore cars near Torneträsk (the lake in the background), in northern Sweden.

Part of the Sovcomflot fleet, the world's largest LNG ice-breaking tanker, the Christophe de Margerie, *set out on its first trip from Sabetta. It can break through 2.1 meters of ice. It made the trip to South Korea in record time.*

cc/kremlin.ru/

first-ever trip of a merchant vessel without ice-breaker escort. These sorts of transits along the whole route of the NSR are still very few.

However, China is investing further westwards in another major development zone, that of the Arkhangelsk region south of Murmansk. In Russia near the borders of Norway and Finland, China's Poly Group Corporation is planning a $5.5 billion development project, involving a new deep-water port and a rail connection to the south (the Belkomur rail project). Coal, mineral fertilizer, oil, timber, ores, construction materials and containers are the main cargo to be transported by the new railway to Arkhangelsk, and reloaded for sea transport at the new port. Igor Orlov, the governor of Arkhangelsk, estimates that the project will generate 40,000 jobs when it is completed in 2023.

The new Murmansk harbor is a node of the intermodal East-West Cargo Transport Corridor connecting China over the land corridors of the New Silk Road with the American East Coast and Great Lakes region. This project was negotiated by the Norwegian consulting company Transportutvikling and the International Railway Union (UIC) with support of the Chinese shipping giant COSCO.

The Arctic Railway in Finland

The easternmost Norwegian port is Kirkenes, which is where the Finnish northern regions seek to connect the Finnish Arctic Railway project. This railway would connect with the famous home town of Santa Klaus, Rovaniemi, in Finland to the south, which is now the northern end-station of the Finnish railways. The Arctic Rail project would open up a big mining region in northern Finland and Sweden for rail transport, whose product could be shipped out north to the Atlantic and NSR, instead of via the Baltic Sea. Kirkenes would also make the NSR itself more economical, because the ice-protected ships classed for going through the NSR, are more expensive when used on the open sea to the west. Kirkenes could offer unloading of the ship cargo for further transport south by rail to continental Europe.

In the south of Finland, there is a Finnish-Estonian plan to build an undersea railway tunnel between Helsinki, Finland, and Tallinn, Estonia. A first feasibility report financed by the EU is expected next month on construction of this so-called FinEst Link by 2050. In November 2017, the Finnish IT billionaire Jan Vesterbacka called for building this 80 km tunnel in just five years, by bringing in Chinese technology and financing. The tunnel would create a region of one mil-

The Poly Group Corporation of China is planning a new deep-water port and a rail project south of Murmansk, Russia.

Close-up photo of the Christophe de Margerie. *part of the Sovcomflot Arctic fleet. Sovcomflot is an experienced operator of ships in the Arctic.*

Sovcomflot/Thomas Nilsen

lion people out of the two capital cities. Its cost is estimated at 13 billion euros. At the same time, the 3 billion euro Arctic Rail project is looking to China for financing. These two projects together will be integrated with the planned 3.6 billion euro Rail Baltica high-speed rail line, which will run from Tallinn to Poland, and there link into Western Europe's rail networks, enabling a direct rail link from Helsinki to Berlin and beyond.

China is already investing in Finnish industry. China's Sunshine Kaidi New Energy Group invested $1.13 billion in a new wood-based biodiesel plant in the northern city of Kemi. More Chinese investments are on the way.

Finland, just having re-elected president Sauli Niinistö, has excellent relations with China. It received China's President Xi Jinping on a state visit in April 2017, the first ever of a Chinese President to Finland. Finland is one of the member states of the Arctic Council (with Russia, the United States, Norway, Sweden, and Denmark) and took over the two-year chairmanship from the USA at the biennial summit in Juneau, Alaska in March 2017. President Xi has arranged for Finland to represent China in meetings of the Arctic Council. Chinese cooperation with the Arctic Council, where China has assumed the status of an observer, is in the center of China's Arctic policy paper mentioned above.

China has been reaching out to the other Scandinavian Arctic nations Norway, Iceland and Denmark, to establish Arctic research facilities on Danish Greenland, the Norwegian island of Spitsbergen, and in Iceland. Strong support from Iceland was important in obtaining observer status for China in the Arctic Council.

The deliberations of the Council have thus far quite successfully avoided efforts to introduce geopolitical conflicts. In fact, U.S. collaboration with Russia in the Arctic, as also in the space program, has been both friendly and mutually beneficial, despite the fact that Obama's 2014 U.S. sanctions on Russia essentially shut down extensive investments by Exxon and other oil companies in the Russian regions of the Arctic—to the detriment of both nations.

NATO member Norway has promoted cooperation with Russia for the development of its "High North," where the exploitation of the energy resources in the Barents Sea was pioneered by the Norwegian oil companies. Norway has been the leading promoter in Europe for the NSR. This is why the world's largest-

cc/Towel401

LNG carriers under construction at the Daewoo Shipbuilding & Marine Engineering (DSME) shipyard in Korea. The Christophe de Margerie *was built by DSME, and is operated by Sovcomflot.*

ever conference on the Arctic, with 3,000-3,500 participants from all over the globe, met Jan. 21-26, 2018, in Tromso, Norway, more than 200 miles north of the Arctic Circle (see article, p. 33).

China's Interest in Scandinavian Infrastructure

Hongkong-based company Sunbase, as a leader of a Chinese consortium, offered to build a new harbor in a fjord north of Gothenburg on the Swedish Atlantic coast in November 2017. It would have the capacity to receive the biggest container ships in the world, which currently have no harbor deep enough in Sweden. This harbor would also be an early stop in Western Europe for the NSR.

The new harbor at the city of Lysekil would have a berth 1,800 meters long and 1,000 meters wide. The plan includes a new bridge, new roads and railways, a terminal for cruise ships, and also urban development. It would be a huge investment in a nation starved for decades of infrastructure development and jobs. It has been welcomed by the city administration, so the Chinese have been asked to present a more detailed plan.

However, the harbor offer has met a storm of protests from the national public radio and other major media, and by locals and security analysts. In the geopolitically-charged climate of Russia-bashing in Sweden, not only Russia, but also China is being attacked for allegedly having colonial and military interests in connection with harbor development projects internationally. The Belt and Road Initiative is being slandered as a policy to project Chinese military and political domination. The participation, in July 2017, of Chinese naval units in military exercises with the Russian fleet in the Baltic Sea, has been highlighted in this debate. The result was that the Chinese consortium announced its decision to pull out of the project on Jan. 30, 2018.

This Swedish China-bashing is very ill conceived, as it could deter Chinese interest in building much-needed Swedish high-speed railway systems. It could also imperil the huge Chinese investments in the Swedish auto sector. Two Chinese industrialists have bought the two Swedish car factories in this region, Volvo Cars, based in Gothenburg, and the former Saab car factory in Trollhattan, where electric-powered cars for China will be produced with the brand name Nevs. On Dec. 27, Volvo Cars owner Geely Holding Group of China, announced it had bought a large minority share (15% in voting rights) in the Swedish truck and construction machine producer Volvo. These Chinese investments in these automotive industries have brought Sweden into one of the world's greatest technology-sharing projects with China.

A Chinese delegation recently visited Norway to discuss the construction of a Chinese-built high-speed rail system from Oslo, Norway, to Stockholm, Sweden, the Norwegian daily *Dagsavisen* reported Jan. 11. The delegation was led by Huang Xin, vice president of the China Association for Promoting International Economic and Technical Cooperation, which is a part of the China Overseas Investment Union. Huang Xin said: "We would be happy to cooperate with Norway and Sweden in this project, both with labor, with our competence, and in contributing to the financing of the project." It is a part of "the Chinese strategy for international investments in infrastructure," Huang Xin said.

The project would cost SEK170 billion (about $20 billion) and reduce the travel time to 2.5 hours. The current railway was built in the 19th century, with very little improvement since. The Norwegian Alf S. Johansen has been promoting this idea for the last five years. He is the coordinator for the EU project TENTacle and head of the secretariat for the border committee for the regional cooperation between the two neighboring regions in Sweden and Norway, Värmland and Östfold. He said to *Dagsavisen* that he had found a very good response from the Chinese. Referring to the "One Belt, One Road," *Dagsavisen* quoted Johansen saying: "With the complete realization of the project, you would go directly from Bergen [Norway] to Moscow and Beijing."

Denmark a Global Maritime Hub

Scandinavian shipping to China is dominated by Denmark and its global container shipping company Maersk. Maersk's background is in the Danish East Asian Company, which dominated Danish business for a hundred years up to the 1990s, when its shipping lines were taken over by Maersk.

On January 22, 2018, the Danish minister of business, Brian Mikkelsen, announced a plan to develop Denmark into a Global Maritime Hub by 2025. The plan, called Blue Denmark, will develop the maritime industry in all parts of the nation. Denmark is already the most China-oriented nation in Europe today. Bilateral trade has increased steadily since the 2008 "strategic partnership" between the two nations. Denmark has the highest proportion of China's trade, 6%, among the Nordic nations, especially because of shipping services from Maersk.

Conclusion

The many China-sponsored projects with the Nordic countries announced in the last months, signify that the Nordic nations finally are starting to open up for China's BRI. These nations, like all of North Western Europe, have been very late to respond to the BRI. When the U.K. applied to become a founding member of the Asian Infrastructure Investment Bank, Denmark also joined, and then Sweden and Norway joined on the last day. It attended the Belt and Road Forum in Beijing (BRF) in May 2017. When, in the very last hours, the British decided to send a minister, then Denmark, Finland and Sweden also joined on a ministerial level on the last day. But no Nordic head of state or government attended the forum. As reported, Finland's President, Sauli Niinistö, received Chinese president Xi Jinping at his home. However, in May, just before BRF, the prime minister of Denmark visited Beijing and President Xi. Then, in June, both the prime ministers of Sweden and Norway went to China to meet him. Important accords were signed, and the fruits of these breakthroughs are now coming in the form of proposals for project cooperation in the whole Arctic region.

The Northern Sea Route of the Maritime Silk Road

by Dean Andromidas and Tony Papert

Jan. 25—The world's largest-ever conference on the Arctic, with 3,000-3,500 participants from all over the globe, is now underway in Tromsø, Norway, more than 200 miles north of the Arctic Circle. Tromsø is famous as the jumping-off point for great Arctic exploration missions, and the center for Arctic hunting in the Nineteenth and Twentieth Centuries.

The focus of interest of the Jan. 21-26 Arctic Frontiers 2018 Conference going on now, is the Northern Sea Route, or the Arctic Route, as an alternative sea route between Europe and Asia. The ongoing melting of the Arctic ice—a phenomenon of the far North not to be confused with non-existent global warming—makes this sea route practicable already today. As *EIR* has reported, Russia is building a series of the world's largest icebreakers in order to expand the use of this route. On June 20, 2017, China officially included the Arctic Route as part of the Maritime Silk Road in its "Vision for Maritime Cooperation under the Belt and Road Initiative."

In an interview with TASS at the conference, Japan's Ambassador for International Economic Affairs, Ambassador for the Japan Year in Russia, and Ambassador in Charge of Arctic Affairs, Keiji Ide, said that Japan was enormously interested in the development of the Northern Sea Route, gas projects in Yamal, and long-term cooperation with Russia.

"Unconditionally, there is enormous interest in the Northern Sea Route. Business people from Hokkaido

Arctic Frontiers 2018/Terje Mortensen

Norwegian Foreign Minister Ine Eriksen Soreide and five other Norwegian government ministers appeared at the Arctic Frontiers conference in Tromso.

A gas facility at the Bovanenkovskoye field in the Yamal gas fields.

were speaking about it at today's conference," said the ambassador, who speaks fluent Russian. "Of course, it is just a beginning. People assess risks and calculate what is profitable or not. They are considering them very carefully."

Ide said there was great interest in the Yamal LNG project, which began last year (which also enjoys significant Chinese investment), as well as the idea of building infrastructure for liquefied natural gas (LNG) production in Russia's Kamchatka Peninsula, in gas fields only 1,730 km northeast of Japan. Ide continued:

> We want to collaborate with our Russian friends pursuing a long-term goal. Regardless of a rift between our countries in politics, we cannot say we do not want to develop our relations. On the contrary, if we come across either difficulties or disagreements, those need to be overcome.
>
> Thank God, your President [Vladimir] Putin and our Prime Minister [Shinzo] Abe enjoy warm, good relations, so we will be developing economic cooperation with Russia.

The independent Russian natural gas giant Novatek was repre-sented in Tromsø by the Norwegian Bjorn Gundersen, Deputy Director of its LNG Projects Department. Novatek's Yamal and associated Murmansk projects are the largest construction projects underway in Russia, and perhaps in the world. Novatek's partner Total (of France) notes on its website:

> At the start of the project, there were no access routes to the site by land or by sea. To facilitate the transportation of equipment and staff, construction began on a large-capacity regional transportation hub in 2011, comprising the port of Sabetta and an international airport.

Shipping LNG in such extreme conditions also required Total and its partners to design a new breed of vessel: the LNG ice-breaker tanker. This innovative solution allows LNG to be transported all year long without the assistance of icebreakers. Measuring 300 meters [in length] and boasting a capacity of 172,600 cubic meters, the ship can sail in ice of up to 2.1 meters thick. In all, 15 LNG ice-breakers will be gradually commissioned between now and 2019, the first of which is the *Christophe de Margerie*.

To unlock access to the vast gas resources of Russia's Far North, the Yamal LNG project has

The first ice-breaking LNG carrier launched in mid-January 2016 in South Korea.

inaugurated a new LNG shipping route. Known as the Northern Sea Route, it enables vessels to reach Asia in 15 days via the Bering Strait, compared with 30 days using the conventional route through the Suez Canal. The journey can be made between May and November, when the ice is thin enough to navigate. This feat is only possible thanks to a new breed of versatile LNG carriers, which feature ice-breaking technology.

The Yamal project's entire LNG production of eventually 34 million tons per year, will all be carried to customers both in Asia and in Europe via the Northern Sea Route.

Alaska Set for Arctic Development

by Marcia Baker

Jan. 27—Alaska Governor Bill Walker proclaimed Jan. 24 that the stars are aligned on Arctic development. Alaska is second to West Virginia in the size of its 2017 Memorandum of Understanding with China, for energy infrastructure and gas sales development—$43 billion over the coming years. Governor Walker met in Fairbanks on Jan. 24 with his cabinet and local mayors, and spoke optimistically about what's ahead, with plans for an 800-mile gas pipeline from the North Slope to Kenai Peninsula. Pledged sales of 75% of the gas is to go to China. Walker was the only governor in the Trump delegation to go to Beijing last November. Walker then hosted President Xi Jinping in Anchorage last May, on Xi's return trip home from Florida.

Walker made a point of praising the support he is getting from the White House. "I could go on for hours about all the different—how things are so different now.... I have a call with the White House about every two weeks, directly with the White House, about this project.... It's astounding, absolutely astounding, to have that kind of relationship with the White House on this project. And then with the market, the producers—the stars are absolutely aligned on this," said Walker, according to a report on Fairbanks' NBC TV affiliate Newscenter 11.

Alaska, working with China, is set to figure prominently in Arctic gas development, as well as the newly opened Yamal, Russia, LNG operations. China covers the principles involved, in its new "Arctic Policy" White Paper, which states explicitly that this is part of its Belt and Road Initiative: China wishes to "advance Arctic-related cooperation under the Belt and Road Initiative in accordance with the basic principles of respect, cooperation, win-win results and sustainability." The document, released Jan. 26, also states specifically under its section "IV. China's Policies and Positions on Participating in Arctic Affairs," that, "China respects the sovereign rights of Arctic States over oil, gas and mineral resources" in the region, and "encourages them to participate in the exploitation of oil, gas, and mineral resources in the Arctic, through cooperation in various forms, on the condition of properly protecting the eco-environment of the Arctic."

Meanwhile, in West Virginia this week, optimistic statements were also made about what's to come from China's commitment to work with the state on gas infrastructure and industry development in Appalachia. At the Jan. 22-23 Economic Development Council Legislative Conference in Charleston, representatives of the major economic associations spoke out on this.

Concretely, announcements are awaited from the governor and Commerce Department on what will be the first projects (regarding a site for a gas hub, for one or more cracker plants, for pipelines, and related infrastructure). No word is out yet on West Virginia Commerce Secretary Woody Thrasher's latest trip to China, which began Jan. 13. Thrasher personally signed the Memorandum of Understanding with China Nov. 9, 2017 in Beijing, for a Chinese commitment of $83.7 billion over 20 years.

The possibilities "are limitless," for West Virginia, said the West Virginia Manufacturers Association President Rebecca McPhail, if China Energy follows through.

The Independent Oil and Gas Association's Executive Director, Charlie Burd, said: "We're very excited to be at the leading edge of what could be a huge economic engine. It's going to be a very exciting time for West Virginia, we believe. It's not going to be overnight. But over the next 5-10 years the landscape of West Virginia has the potential to change dramatically."

June 4, 2010

THIS PRESENT CENTURY

The Secret Economy's Outlook

by Lyndon H. LaRouche, Jr.

What I had named "The Secret Economy" has four crucial elements: **a.) An urgently needed, revolutionary re-definition of an implicitly, dynamically orderable series of universal economic principles of infrastructure; b.) A fresh definition of universal physical space-time, restating the intention of the Mendeleyev periodic table in terms of a universal system of cosmic radiation; c.) A new, scientific definition of the noetic quality of physical-economic function of "basic economic infrastructure" consistent with the enhanced view of the ontological characteristic of physical space-time; and d.) A needed redefinition of the term "economy" by a relevant, universal physical principle, done through a reform which identifies the human personal identity in terms of the creative potential of the specifically human mind, rather than as being regarded elementarily by a notion identified in terms of mere sense-perception.**

Now, once each of those four categories had been considered, the next step would be a series of publications which introduce the reader to what must become adopted as the underlying principles of **a science of physical economy**. *What will be presented in this fashion, will represent the needed programmatic political outcome for rescuing the planet from the present immediate threat of a global "dark age" now descending rapidly on our planet as a whole.*

The result of this series of reports will become, in effect, a new way of looking at the human species itself, a new practical way of seeing man's newly defined, proper role in the universe, and of defining it in a practical way, the actual, future meaning of human life, as our species moves outward to include the occupation of other parts of our Solar system and into the larger scope of this galaxy and beyond.

The Friedrich Nietzsche who had not only died a horrible death, but a disgusting one, had said: "God is dead!" Nietzscheans today add nothing in this matter which Aristotle had not said earlier in denying the continued existence of both God's and human creativity in the universe. President Barack Obama and his cohorts are walking in the shadow of not only Paolo Sarpi, but that of the deceased Nietzsche; the toleration of Obama's kind of misleadership is typical of what is really wrong with the world's economy, when taken as a whole, right now.

Introduction

Thus far, the relevant, probably best guess available to us, on the subject of economy, is that the concept of "universe" must be considered as if our universe had been generated by the creative powers which have been placed at the disposal of mankind. This should be read as echoed in the context of the past practices of relatively frequent, stellar modes of transoceanic navigation, during some past time such as either the most recent of the planet's presently known great ice-ages, or a still earlier such age. Such findings from known evidence are coherent with what the ancient so-called "Greek," Egyptian, and Pythagorean maritime cultures knew in respect to the subjects of "Sphaerics," of *dynamis*, and of the general knowledge of Pythagoreans such as Archytas. Such, for example, is the knowledge possessed by Plato, as typified by his celebrated illustration of this point in his **Parmenides** dialogue.

The same emphasis bearing on a principle of universal coherence, is to be recognized within today's broader sphere of the broader, modern European cultures, as expressed by such developments set as the pattern in the modern discoveries launched by such as Filippo Brunelleschi and Nicholas of Cusa, or by work of such followers of Plato and Cusa as Leonardo da Vinci, and by the Johannes Kepler who contributed his uniquely original discovery of a principle of universal, physical gravitation.

Such is the method which has led to what my "basement" associates have come to identify as the implications of the modern principled notion of that "cosmic radiation" through which man's existence interacts, more and more knowledgeably, with the cosmic forces of the universe, not only on a broader galactic scale, but even beyond.

However, above and beyond all that, it is our deepened conception of the individual member of mankind itself which must, already, now, impel us into a process of a succession of radical changes in our understanding of the true nature and destiny of our human species and the economy on which it depends, both within the universe, and, therefore, ourselves.

The Pazzi Chapel in Florence, designed by Filippo Brunelleschi (1377-1446).

For the occasion of this present report, I shall define the most applicable expression of Gottfried Leibniz's notion of what was to be developed further as a Riemannian *analysis situs*, as I have applied this to define the elementary principles of a science of physical economy, that as a notion in accord with Leibniz's late 1690s notion of *dynamics*, his treatment of the physical principle of least action. In the case immediately at hand, I do so from the specific standpoint of that especially relevant part of the work of Niels Abel and Lejeune Dirichlet which bears on a specifically Riemannian treatment of the topic of *analysis situs* for this case.

Admittedly, since Leibniz's original statement on this subject, there have been numerous, chiefly mutually contradictory usages of the term "analysis situs." Rather than taking the reader of this present report through a swamp of wildly conflicting definitions of that term by sundry varieties of specialists, I shall focus on an implied definition which is consistent with the intent of Leibniz and with the contributions to Bernhard Riemann's principle by such Nineteenth-century figures as Abel and Dirichlet. My chief reference on this account, is to the extremely profound relevance of the

Leibniz notion of *least action* for the case of a science of physical economy. I employ a notion of physical (rather than mathematical) notion of least action, a notion which is consistent, in its primitive expression, with the elementary form of the physical principle of the catenary function (and, also, Leibniz's concept of *dynamics*).

I cross-reference that to Albert Einstein's introduction of the notion of a finite, but not bounded universe, as Einstein defined this as implicit in Johannes Kepler's **Harmonies**. The case of the elementary form of the catenary is crucial for us as illustrating that conception.

That is to add the following.

To illustrate the case, choose two selected, related points in physical-economic space-time, and follow the relevant function expressed by this process, as between those points as they implicitly bound the efficiently physical relationship among those points (i.e., *analysis situs*). That is to say, in the relationship among the cohering participants in the apparently finite space of the physical function performed between those points.

I.e., consider the catenary as defined, as it had been defined as a physical principle of Filippo Brunelleschi's design of construction of the Florence Cathedral's cupola, and also the Pazzi Chapel. Adjust this image for the effects of a rate of change in the parameters of the process as a whole. This signifies, of course, that all the relevant aspects of the process, as defined by the bounds of this illustration, have a common function, in *analysis situs*, which is integral with that indicated effect.

I. The Ontological Issue of Economy

Probably, we should consider the first observation to be proffered for a physical-economic process, by illustrations of the type which combine the apparent elements of what appear to be a collection of the type which Plato treated in his masterly ridicule of the reductionist Parmenides. The solutions to problems of such a type, are typical of a process which is to be considered from the top, down, of that array, as being, *ontologically,* characteristically *dynamic* in the sense of Leibniz's unique creation of any legitimate modern use of that term. What should be considered as the model for defining a dynamic process of change in *analysis situs* modeling of a typical real (physical) economy, is one which becomes subject to competent analysis only when approached from that standpoint in method of composition.

A suitable classroom illustration of that notion, is provided by considering the interval during which the economy of the Massachusetts Bay Colony operated within the terms of the design of a *credit* system for the role of the Pinetree Shilling, rather than as a *monetary* system, as that opposition to monetarism was practiced during a time preceding the British monarchy's crushing of the colony's charter.

For example:

The actually relevant components of an economy,[1] are comprised of *basic economic infrastructure, agriculture,* and *manufacturing*, each and all of which *are properly subsumed by the role of the related, noëtic functions of both Classical artistic composition* and *physical science.*

Each of these three primary components, in turn, would be described foolishly, if considered by some modern "Parmenides," instead of the standpoint of some virtual modern "Plato." Treated separately thus,

each of these elements would not be suited for being combined according to a common single principle of action. Contrary to a modern "Parmenides," any really successful modern economy, is one which can be shown as efficiently expressing a single, subsuming, unifying principle of such three categories of constituent aspects. Such is the leading implication of Leibniz's uniquely original definition of modern *dynamics*.

'The Post-War Schumpeter Syndrome'

For example: consider the physical fact, that from the date of President Franklin Roosevelt's death, the U.S. economy has never achieved a truly functional net physical-economic growth, per capita and per square kilometer, to the present day. Consider the way in which Joseph Schumpeter's frankly Nietzschean notion of "creative destruction" was employed under President Harry Truman to shrink what had become the employed productive capacity of what had been the war-time physical economy of the U.S.A. This was done under the Truman regime's capitulation to an anti-Franklin Roosevelt promotion of a post-war restoration of British and related imperialisms. The result of that Truman policy, was the draining of what should have become the productive potential of the post-war world, as this was effected through Churchill's drawing Truman into what became Bertrand Russell's 1946 doctrine of the "preventive nuclear war" Russell proposed to be launched against the Soviet Union, a war which Russell intended should establish a system of world government like that intended by the British empire today.

As the Nietzschean doctrine of Schumpeter forerunner Werner Sombart emphasized, prolonged, wasting war, is the principal link of Schumpeter to Nietzsche on this account.

The pattern of continuing, post-"World War II" destruction in world economy, has largely depended upon both the so-called "Cold War" launched under Winston Churchill's "Iron Curtain" slogan, and the protracted warfare characteristic of the entire period since. Thus, the post-1945 result of burdening the economy with useless forms of long wars, and related effects of organized activities, non-activities, and expenditures, has been fostered by aid of such insane economic doctrines as that of Schumpeter's notion of "creative destruction" and its like. The "bail out" of Wall Street types of hyperinflationary violations of a "Glass-Steagall" principle, has been merely typical of such public, and sometimes also pubic insanity.

---

1. E.g., without gambling permitted.

The 'Gale' of Creative Destruction

Friedrich Nietzsche (1844-1900), the conceptual father of "creative destruction."

Werner Sombart (1863-1941) coined the term that Schumpeter later adopted.

Joseph Schumpeter (1883-1950), author of The Process of Creative Destruction, *1942.*

World Economic Forum/swiss-image.ch/E.T. Studhalter

Larry Summers, currently the top economic advisor to President Obama, wrote in the early 2000s that "the economy of the future is likely to be 'Schumpeterian.'"

Creative Commons/Allan Warren

Lord Harold Wilson's destruction of the already shaky British economy, as prime minister (1974-76), is a classic case of the application of Schumpeter's doctrine.

Joseph Schumpeter described his Nietzschean notion of "creative destruction" thusly: "The opening up of new markets and the organizational development from the craft shop and factory to such concerns as US Steel illustrate the process of industrial mutation that incessantly revolutionizes the economic structure from within, incessantly destroying the old one, incessantly creating a new one. . . . [The process] must be seen in its role in the perennial gale of creative destruction. . . ."

The case of British Prime Minister Harold Wilson, is among the notable instances of the British policies of "creative destruction." Wilson launched his campaign to this effect under the opportunities afforded by the 1963 assassination of U.S. President John F. Kennedy, for the launching of the ruinous, 1964-1975 U.S. war in Indo-China. Wilson's leading role in the "creative destruction" of the already shaky British economy, is a clinically "classical case" in the application of Schumpeter's cultish doctrine.

As in all extended periods of genuine crisis, as in the recurring, 1963-1975 span, from the wave of assassination attempts against France's President Charles de Gaulle, and the assassination of President John F. Kennedy, until the close of the official U.S. warfare in Indo-China. Include the case of the assassination of Britain's Dr. David Kelly, as part of clearing away opposition to Prime Minister Tony Blair's fraudulent pretext for launching the vastly ruinous effects on the U.S.A. of a prolonged long, wasting war in Southwest Asia's Iraq.

In real history, it is never events which direct the course of history, but, rather, the implicitly inhering intent of those policies which generate and shape great events.

The Science of Society

There is a definable function, consistent with Leibniz's original notion of *dynamics*, which steers a positive outcome for a wide assortment of necessary expenditures on various expressions of public administration, basic economic infrastructure, manufacturing, and agriculture, this on the condition that an increasingly capital-intensive emphasis on science-driven, and Classical-art-driven progress is operating. The function which "recognizes" such an arrangement efficiently, is an expression of a Riemannian, anti-positivist practice of *analysis situs*, as Leibniz defined the only competent attributions of such terms as *analysis situs* and *dynamics*.

As Leibniz and Jean Bernouilli had already shown, during their close collaboration, in their defining a notion of a universal least action as a principle of physical economy, the principle, that the catenary as such is merely an elementary form of expression for a higher order of a function of physical least action. Nonetheless, that view of the principle of the catenary as a pedagogical device, also remains the germ of the pedagogy needed for guiding students and others toward the more advanced outgrowths of that notion, Leibniz's original notion of a literally dynamic principle of least action, in the sense of the ancient Classical notion of *dynamis*, or Leibniz's introduction of the physical conception known as *dynamics*.

It is not conceivable on the basis of any relevant evidence of which I have been informed, that the underlying principles of the actually principled form of relevant, ancient scientific method, could have been discovered, except through the development of a functional concept of astronomy derived from no less than many centuries of the practice of stellar methods of trans-oceanic navigation by continuously functioning maritime cultures of the type which coincide with prolonged "ice age" intervals. What is called "The Great Platonic Cycle" which Bal Gangadhar Tilak attributed, in his **Orion**, to a central-Asian (pre-Sanskrit) Vedic language-culture living in Central Asia more than 6,000 years ago. That cycle is the briefest (about 25,000 years) of the three principal cycles of a long-ranging, compound Solar cycle. It is otherwise known as the Platonic cycle, as attributed knowledge of Plato during his own lifetime.

It is also the case, that competent discussion of the catenary and its seminal implications, remains an indispensable phase of introduction of the students to the more correct, more advanced conceptions of the required elementary principles of practice of physical economy.

This coheres with the notions of the Egypt and related sources of the science of *Sphaerics* associated with such as the Pythagoreans, and thus with the great Archytas and his associate Plato.

See that aspect of a science of physical economy in the following way.

How an Economy Works

The practice of a typical economy experiences the historical simultaneity of two opposing social tendencies. On the one hand, relatively more successful nations and their economies tend to consume those relatively richest assets which ensure the currently highest relative rate of gain of physical productivity per capita and per square kilometer, this in the specific case in which a successful economy produces increases in the rate of productivity, per capita and per square kilometer, that to what should be the intended effect of a net physical gain for that society, per capita and per square kilometer.

Those net gains, if they do occur in fact, incur two principal incremental costs of an upward net movement. The first of these costs, is a factor of depletion customarily inhering in the earlier stage of the system; the second factor of cost, is the increased expenditure of per capita consumption which must be recognized as the price of an increase in a needed margin of gain in absolute rates of productivity per capita and per square kilometer. The margin of net gain, if it occurs, is in excess of such nominal increases in elements of costs, a development which is generated as a net benefit of anti-entropic gains in human productivity.[2]

The most typical factor of improvement of productivity, both per capita and per square kilometer of territory, is an increase of what has been, for relatively successful branches of expressed cultures, a usually science-driven, relative gain in specific energy-flux-density, which that part of mankind (i.e., society) employs as the basis for the practice of its technology.

There are two exemplary, principal sources of progress to be considered. One is typified by mankind's dependency upon the essential, natural benefits of the increased role of "carbon," as through the principled form of action by chlorophyll (and also the replacement of the role of the magnesium ion in chlorophyll by an alternative such as copper) in transforming relative deserts (or oceans) as into such benefits as blooming forests. The other is typified by human creative ingenuity. The net increase of the combined effect, as when man intervenes to promote the growth of the role of carbon, chlorophyll, and human will and the like, is potentially greater than gains in any, by each of these which might be considered as acting independently of the others of kindred types.[3]

The latter cases, including that of chlorophyll, are typifications of the anti-entropic role which is charac-

2. The relevant, modern, contrary view of economy, such as the British system the British followers of Paolo Sarpi dictated to Karl Marx at the British Museum, denies the existence of any knowable physical principle in economy, other than the infantile, statistical, *post hoc, ergo propter hoc* doctrine of such as Adam Smith and Jeremy Bentham's imperialist school.

3. Calcium, iron, and copper, typify roles kindred to that indicated here for chlorophyll.

The use of solar panels on a large scale is morally and otherwise insane; instead, use the combined tools of chlorophyll and improved irrigation potential for desert areas! Left: a solar array in Waldpolenz, Germany; right: irrigation of lettuce near Phoenix, Ariz.

to, respectively, non-living, living, and human phase-spaces within the universe, is of a form which defines these spaces as functionally interactive. Not only are such living and non-living chemistries interactive, but as the development of the science of physical chemistry has demonstrated, increasingly, since the work of such as Pasteur and Mendeleyev, the interaction among the respective phase-spaces is often positive, even indispensable.

In the practice of economy, mankind discovers and frequently employs the powers of anti-entropy associated with both living and non-living processes, and uses those discoveries in a more or less willful way, as in an historically very large part of the gains which man's will promotes as an essential part of the net productive gains in human net productivity.

Therefore, we should rightly regard the use of solar panels on a large scale as morally and otherwise insane, when the combined tools of chlorophyll and improved irrigation potential should be used, instead. Irrigate the relatively desert regions, for the promotion of the development of local environments for the use of chlorophyll in cooling overheated climates, to transform hot desert areas into a cooled green, and also provide the infrastructural basis for the maintenance and increase of human productivity in general.

teristic of living processes, as this is expressed by the process of evolutionary emergence of higher forms of animal life. The creative powers uniquely specific to mankind among all living species presently known in the universe, are uniquely willful; that is the distinction between the expressions of anti-entropic principles of development by willful act of human creativity, and the qualitatively lower quality of anti-entropy which is not only specific to all other forms of life, but which is also expressed as typical among non-living qualities of processes in a more general way.[4]

This separation among the characteristics specific

II. History as Scientific Method

Within the concluding section of an earlier publication **The Secret Economy**,[5] I presented what had been a little known, but actual relationship between *consciousness as merely an expression of sense-percep-*

---

4. For example, it is through the action of relevant living processes, that V.I. Vernadsky's Biosphere provides a crucial part of what society is enabled to harvest as what present habits identify as "ores."

5. "What Your Accountant Never Understood: The Secret Economy," **EIR**, May 28, 2010.

tion, and *a higher order of consciousness*, one which has been, usually, rarely formed in the individual human mind up to the present day, but which remains, nonetheless, as the essential basis for fostering of actually willful creativity within, or among human individuals.

My aim here, on that account, is to promote an increase in the awareness of, and power to employ that higher order of creative powers of the human mind, so to reverse what, in fact, has been the declining degree of relevant attention to such matters over the course of the post-World War II period of the steep decline in the knowledge of what had been Classical culture. Now, here, I aim to bring into being that higher standpoint of human consciousness which had been, chiefly, lost during what is now approaching the magnitude of four recent generations of trans-Atlantic society, in particular.

In this way, what I emphasize here, is a power of the human mind which we may tend to view as, heretofore, usually limited to the persons of the greatest scientists and poets, and that, chiefly, during what had been those relatively exceptional past times and cultures known from relatively most fortunate times and places of history past.

It is convenient, in the process of discussing this aspect of science for its bearing on matters of physical science of economy, that we should employ the notion of a qualitative distinction between, first, the functions of the "brain," and, second, the relatively higher, *Leibnizian dynamic*, functions of what can be fairly identified as "the human mind" *—or, in other words, the human soul*.[6]

Although the awareness of the full implications of that categorical distinction, is rare among recent generations, up to the present day, the shadowy effects of a merely "pre-conscious" expression of the functions of "mind," are to be located in the observable form of expressions of occasional surges of potential creativity, expressed as "a flash of insightfulness" among members of populations in which the habit of practice of progress is encouraged.

The quality of an emotion of "love," expressed as humanism, as by the Apostle Paul in his **I Corinthians** 13, rather than sexual passion, reflects that quality of

"pre-consciousness" which lies within the same ontological domain as those human impulses specific to love of mankind. This distinction excludes both the love of a thing, and the attributable aspect of "thingness" to a person or persons. As this point shall become clearer as we proceed here, it is a matter of the immortal relationship of one mind-as-such to another mind-assuch, not to a mere object of sense-perception.

The distinction toward which I have just pointed here, will be made clearer, in the course of this present chapter, once we have come to share my view of the higher meaning of the notion of "mind."

I have thought it necessary to pose the question in this form now, in order that I might better convey *the crucial emotional distinction* between the experience of sense-perception and the actually human, higher category of experience associated with the proper notion of mind.

In **The Secret Economy**, I had emphasized the aspect of falseness in all blindly literal readings of sense-perception as such. There was nothing fanciful in my making that distinction; it is the conception which underlies the discovery of the essential principle of competent modern science, as in Nicholas of Cusa's **De Docta Ignorantia**, and by such among Cusa's successors as Leonardo da Vinci, Johannes Kepler, Gottfried Leibniz, the polymath Abraham Kästner, and Bernhard Riemann's seminal, 1854 habilitation dissertation. It was also the quality often expressed by Albert Einstein, as in the instance of Einstein's unique insight into the principle of Johannes Kepler's uniquely original discovery of the universal principle of gravitation.

That much said on this just stated area of investigation, I now focus, as I had done in my **The Secret Economy**, on that crucial feature of Kepler's discovery of gravitation to which Einstein referred in his own, crucial commentary on Kepler's discovery.

In **The Secret Economy**, my argument on this specific subject of the human mind, had proceeded along the following lines.

What are customarily denoted as the different qualities among sense-perceptions, each fail the believer, that in each instance taken by itself.

The case of Helen Keller illustrates the nature of the issue posed. It is in the mind, that mankind may find efficient means of access to conceptualization of the real universe which we inhabit; but, it is not bounded within those functions of perception traced merely to the brain's relationship to mere sense-perceptions. The

---

6. The relevance of this use of the term "soul" will be made clearer in the course of the unfolding of the content of this chapter. There are no errant liberties which have been taken in stating the matter in these terms.

principal discoveries of a great follower of Cardinal Nicholas of Cusa, Johannes Kepler, are of crucial importance for our reference to that subject here.

The deficiency of sense-perception as such, is typified by the modern, Liberal followers of Paolo Sarpi, such as that follower of the Liberal school, Pierre-Simon Laplace. Laplace, with the folly of his Liberal's reductionist view of the Solar system, was never able to comprehend Kepler's uniquely original discovery of the knowable physical principle of universal gravitation. Nor, in fact, did any of the Liberal school desire to actually make that re-discovery, even when all the conclusive evidence has been available to them in detail from Kepler's published work.

Thus, the only true and original form of discovery of the actual principle of gravitation, has been that of Kepler, as in the detailed account of that discovery given by his **Harmonies**.[7] Albert Einstein's appreciation of Kepler's unique achievement is crucial for insight into the subject-matter which we take up in this present chapter of my report.

Ask yourself: why would a professedly leading astronomer, Laplace, who had sufficient relevant work of Kepler available to him, fail to present a competent account of the function of universal gravitation? The formal explanation of Laplace's folly, is elementary: he never considered that crucial proof of Kepler's discovery, which is to be found in Kepler's published statements on that matter. I bring it up here because Laplace's folly goes so clearly to the root of the kinds of fraud introduced against not only Leibniz and Kepler, but many relevant others, as by the Eighteenth-century and early Nineteenth-century followers of Rene Descartes, Leonhard Euler, Pierre-Simon Laplace, Augustin Cauchy, et al.

Why did Laplace disgrace himself in this manner? Essentially, his error then was echoed by what Britain's J.C. Maxwell said later, when asked why he never seemed to know any of the crucial actual discoveries on which the work of such essential predecessors as Gauss, Weber, and Riemann had been based. Maxwell did reply in an as if implicit defense of Laplace later: *We (British Liberals) never considered any scientific work but [that which agreed with] our own.*[8]

That kind of behavior should not surprise anyone familiar with relevant matters of science. The same fraudulent treatment of subject-matters of physical principle, is all too typical of that virtual Babylonian priesthood constituted from among the "peer review" agencies largely relied upon, still today, for such purposes as controlling education in schools and universities today. I have repeatedly experienced the opinion of those prominent professors of physical science, from both sides of the Atlantic, who simply deny crucial and conclusive matters of scientific evidence, with the same kind of fraud so frankly admitted by Maxwell.[9]

Here, once I have said that much about Maxwell and his like, the remaining particular significance of Laplace's willful hoax itself, is that anyone who accepts that particular hoax, is rendered a case of self-inflicted lack of capacity for understanding the higher faculties of the human mind.

So, it is essential to emphasize, that Kepler's discovery of the principle of gravitation, is based on a crucial-experimental demonstration of the contradictory evidence supplied by the role of the sense of vision per se, and the contrary implications of harmonics.

Once we have comprehended that much, we should find ourselves led from the particular subject of the principle of gravitation, very quickly, to the broader notion of principle-in-general, which I am presenting in this chapter.

Ask oneself: Is it not the case, from "walking through" the fact of Kepler's actually original discovery of the universal principle of gravitation, that the entire range of mankind's natural and synthetic forms of sense-perceptual experience, could no longer be regarded as a source of scientific, or Classical-artistic "sense-certainty" respecting the principles which

---

7. The attribution of a discovery of gravitation to Isaac Newton, was always a hoax, and was known to be such among competent British scientists during Newton's lifetime, through evidence which notorious dilettantes of British court-circles put aside at that time. By the early decades of Nineteenth Century, each and every claim to a discovery of a principle by Newton had been fully discredited, yet, throughout the entirety of the Nineteenth Century, and, largely, up to the present day, the silly Newton of the myth created by Abbé Antonio S. Conti, persists as a kind of heathen religious devotion, on some issues, such as the subject of gravitation, among even some otherwise accomplished, but fearful scientists. Among the latter, the sheer fraud of the followers of Bertrand Russell and the International Institute for Applied Systems Analysis of Russell's Cambridge circles, is the worst case.

8. Laplace and his accomplice Augustin Cauchy were brought in to replace the Ecole Polytechnique's Gaspard Monge and Lazare Carnot through the British controller of occupied France at that time, the Duke of Wellington.

9. E.g. the frauds against both science and mankind, such as those expressed as promotion of "cap and trade" legislation peddled to dupes today.

govern the real universe which we inhabit?

That is not to imply that there is no element of what we might regard as "reason" in the functions of human sense-perception. Rather, the exemplary case of Kepler's uniquely original discovery of the principle of universal gravitation, demonstrates that, contrary to the Liberalism of Paolo Sarpi, we must regard sense-perception as such, as Kepler did in discovering the principle of gravity: *as presenting us with shadows cast by reality.* Careful use of powers of sense-perception confronts the competent scientific worker with those paradoxes, known as crucial ontological conflicts, the mere shadows cast by unseen reality, which serve as the clues of irony which reveal the presence of a likely universal physical principle, just as Kepler discovered the general principle of Solar gravitation.

Once we have come that far, the next step must be to conceptualize that which has cast such a shadow.

Thus, for as long as we continue the error of believing that the cast shadows called sense-perception, are reality as such, we substitute what are merely truly shadows for that reality which has cast the shadows. Ask oneself: *what, then, is the remedy for this still, presently, commonplace error in human judgment still today?*

Then, ask: Why, perhaps, did Leipzig's Abraham Kästner dedicate his adult life to the cause of Gottfried Leibniz and Johann Sebastian Bach? Why did the same Kästner, a leading figure in Eighteenth-century science at Göttingen in his time, also play a leading personal role at the center of backing for the American political cause of Benjamin Franklin, as a backer of his own protégé Gotthold Lessing, and backer of the Lessing-Moses Mendelssohn collaboration against the enemies of Leibniz's tradition, and also play a crucial role in rescuing an authentic Shakespeare from the neglected virtual tomb to be found in an Eighteenth-century, British cultural rubbish-field?

The proper answer to such questions may be summarized as follows.

Me & Percy Bysshe Shelley

My deceased friend and collaborator, one of the last, relatively few, really professional American historians remaining from the practice of university faculties in his time, H. Graham Lowry, Graham, dedicated the last decades of his life, from about 1983 onward, as he described it to me in making the proposal for the production of his book on the subject of the necessarily exist-

ing bridge within the 1630-1754 period. He linked the golden age of Massachusetts' Seventeenth Century and its renaissance which emerged during the Eighteenth Century, to uncovering the bridge which had been the means of transition toward the victory of the American Revolution.[10]

The nature of Graham's discovery emerged for my knowledge from the day he and his wife came into my Leesburg, Virginia office of that time, to report that he had pin-pointed Gottfried Leibniz's role inside England during part of the period of Queen Anne's reign. Where had Leibniz nearly succeeded in preventing the degeneration of England under the then scheduled transformation to a British monarchy? What Graham pin-pointed was what he described to me as "the missing link" between the revolutionary achievements in statecraft of the Massachusetts Bay colony under its original charter, prior to England's Seventeenth-century crushing of the Massachusetts charter, and the resumption of that effort by such American patriots as the Benjamin Franklin who emerged as a leader of the revival of that cause which came to be associated with the role of leadership provided by Franklin. Graham's known professional competence as an historian, and hearing his summary of his discovered evidence on that occasion, left me no doubt of either the merit, or the importance of the proposed project.

However, there is more to that story. Graham's project also touched me in what has turned out to be of considerable importance for me personally, as also professionally. That story is highly relevant to my subject in this present chapter; it runs as follows.

Already, at the time of Graham Lowry's indicated visit to my office, I was already significantly aware of a certain part of the antiquity of my own family's existence in North America, something which I knew through my knowledge since childhood, of a well-known trace which turned up in the published family record of the Lancaster family inside North America, that in addition to my acquaintance with grandparents born during the 1860s, and my knowledge of a family ancestry in Canada and Scotland from about the time of my grandparents' grandparents. The now recent publication of a scholarly study of my family tree under the direction of relevant British professional historians in

---

10. H. Graham Lowry, *How The Nation Was Won: America's Untold Story 1630-1754*, (Washington, D.C.: Executive Intelligence Review, 1987).

such matters, showed the additional fact of an ancestor's part in the landing at Plymouth, as part of those who arrived on the Mayflower.

For me, that history from 1620 through to the present day, is not a chronicle of events, but is, rather, history read as reflections of a lawfully continuing process of development over what is presently a span of history of but one decade shy of three centuries. It is a process of accumulation of often seemingly kaleidoscopic changes. It is an experience which flows as the continuity of a living process in its own right, rather than the implicitly kinematic series of percussive actions seen by the unfortunately, credulous (and, usually, also hysterical) perverts whose litany is, "there are no conspiracies in history."

The point of emphasizing that matter here, is that the latter finding of my family's connection to 1620, pinned down facts of considerable relevance to the subject of this present report. This bears on a fact which is highly relevant to the subject of this report, the subject identified by Percy Bysshe Shelley's **A Defence of Poetry**. The implications of Shelley's argument are *dynamic* according to Leibniz's definition of that term.

It is said by experts in that field, that if we tame the young puppy of a wild dog at an appropriate age, the progeny of that dog as an adult will tend to be civilized by dog owners' standards, especially when properly reared as "a family dog."[11] However, what happens with human beings, rather than other species, is of a type which Shelley identifies in the concluding paragraphs of his **A Defence of Poetry**.

The principle which Shelley's account references, is a reflection of the conception of *dynamics* which Gottfried Leibniz had developed during the 1690s. It is that same phenomenon which I have identified, earlier in this chapter, as that aspect of the human mind which is associated with an innate, specifically human creativity which lies outside the realm of those aspects of human

Creative Commons/German Federal Archive/Bernd Settnik

The mass-strike process in Germany (shown here in Berlin, Nov. 4, 1989), led to the collapse of the communist state. We live today in similarly tumultuous times, with the potential for dramatic change.

mental life which are associated with ordinary sense-certainty.

It is that same principle of social dynamics which is consistent with that of Leibniz, which Rosa Luxemburg referenced with the phenomenon of "the mass strike," the same phenomenon which has been increasingly apparent in the patterns of mass behavior of U.S. citizens since the outbreak of Congressional meetings with constituents during August 2009. It is also, ominously, the same ominous phenomenon witnessed in the former (east) German Democratic Republic in the *"Wir sind das Volk,"* in Leipzig and elsewhere, which led into the collapse of that state.

At some times in past history, there are rather sudden upsurges of ominous mass phenomena which have taken root even in experiences from ancient times. Here, we touch upon a quality of experience which points toward a notion of immortality, a notion sprung from deep-rooted ideas, ideas which date to even much earlier generations, as if the dead have arisen from their graves to clamor for justice long denied, even during a lapse of many earlier generations. Such developments bring on moments during which tyrants must tremble, and kingdoms may be felled by a lurking, pent-up, sudden expression of the popular will.

We live in precisely such ominous times as those, that more or less world-wide, now.

So, after the charter of the Massachusetts Bay

---

11. Admittedly, I must give way to my wife's competence in such matters; but, the facts I present are true.

colony had been nullified by the British monarchy, under the successive roles of James II and William of Orange, there was a moment of ongoing history in which the intervention of Leibniz, on the ground in England during that time, planted the seeds which would soon sprout in sundry locations in North America, preparing the way for an Eighteenth Century American revolution which would shake the foundations of the world's civilizations. What had proved to be, unfortunately, an abortive moment under the reign of Queen Anne, sparked by Leibniz's intervention then, was, as Graham Lowry has shown, to erupt as an American Revolution which transformed the trans-Atlantic world, and which gave birth to the decisive historic moment of the victorious United States at Yorktown.

Nearly a century after 1776, the specter of the mass-strike returned with great force, under the leadership of President Abraham Lincoln, and would, yet again, with a comparable effect of renewal under President Franklin Roosevelt. It is now mobilizing in preparation to strike, again, now.

The present times are more than over-ripe for a similar affirmation of the succession of the Plymouth landing and the Massachusetts Bay colony. Let all tyrants tremble accordingly. Rosa Luxemburg's "mass strike" is afoot in such a manner, now. Leibniz's "dynamics" is thus displaying its flourishes, now.

So, when I examine certain manifested states of mind, especially those reflections which bear on the principles expressed in the form of a likeness of spirit to great Classical poetry, or, to genuinely creative discoveries of physical-scientific practice, as in New England under the Massachusetts Bay charter, I am often able to recognize the origin of something within myself which has no other genesis than something echoed from somewhere amid even centuries past of our society's history. I can also see a similar experience embodied in others. In such a fashion, we may partake of that prescience of immortality within our own conscience, the same prescience which marks the true American historian.

Such are the intimations of immortality expressed as the ominous closing paragraphs of Shelley's **A Defence of Poetry**.

That is a phenomenon akin to the celebrated, and, in fact, crucial paradox posed by the scientist Louis-Victor de Broglie, as that bears on the work of Max Planck and Planck's close intellectual associates earlier. I explain, as follows.

Substance, or Shadow?

Once we confess the reality of the fact, that what we may have experienced, at some current times, as if it were a mere sense-perception, may, actually, also be the expression of a shadow cast by a more ancient reality, rather being an event which has now reflected the more powerful influence of the ominous shadow from the past.[12] In such a case, we are impelled to "look at" the universe in a qualitatively different way than might the stubborn adherent of the schools of simply sense-certainty. The paradox posed by Kepler's uniquely original discovery of the principle of universal gravitation, is exemplary.

The first step to be taken, once we have gained that much of the territory of experience into which we are entering, is to examine ourselves and our experience, from the vantage-point of the higher-ranking character of those changes in expressed historical principle which lend a new quality of existence to the mere chronicle of events. Such is the standpoint which one must accept in viewing the onrush of the general, planet-wide economic-breakdown-crisis currently in progress during the presently onrushing weeks, toward a most critical phase, a phase significantly comparable to that of Weimar Germany during the Summer and early Autumn of 1923.

Once we accept that quality of evidence, such as that implicitly comparable to what was presented by the concluding phases of Johannes Kepler's successful discovery of the physical principle of gravitation, we must look at ourselves in a special way.

Do the following.

Imagine yourself as to be viewed in the guise of an object (e.g., a shadow) of a person occupied with that his or her experience of mere sense-perceptions as such. So, when you think that you perceive yourself as being what is actually such a shadow, such a mere object of sense-perception, so you are also acting with the motives you attribute to that mere shadow, at least to the extent you locate yourself within the same domain in which your superstitious perceptions argue

---

12. I must take this moment as the relevant occasion to denounce, as contemptible practice, the use of stage-costuming of past history in contemporary attire. The abuse of Shakespeare by such anachronism, as by Orson Welles' Mercury Theater, is typical of the theater which would costume the players in a winter scene in the Arctic, as nudists. The mind of the audience must reckon with the distance of the time and place from the reality of the time and place to which the mind of the audience is to be referenced.

is the actually experienced reality.

Hold that image of your self-deception in view!

Let the real you, the one you can not see directly in an act of sense-perception as such, now look at your shadow, which you are now casting. Where, then, do you find "the real you" who corresponds, thus, to the real, unseen, ontologically substantial universe, a universe which expresses itself by such means as through the actual principle of gravitation as projected by Kepler?

The obvious question posed by that paradox, is "Can you discover the means by aid of which you might actually 'see' the 'real you' in that configuration?" No; you can not. "Do you know that the unseen 'real you' who is 'seeing' what is actually only the shadow of you, actually exists?" Yes, you can know that. "How, then?" By the method of crucial experiments used for the discovery of universal principles. Look over the shoulder of Albert Einstein while Einstein is describing the universe which he recognizes, in Kepler's discovery, as "finite, but unbounded." It is the real universe, which no empiricist, no mere statistician, could ever know.

Art & Science

Compare this with a comparable challenge from the domain of Classical musical composition. Take, as a sample, two specially related compositions of W.A. Mozart: first, his "Ave Verum Corpus," which was a relatively very late work in his life-time, a composition which is to be compared with his important, earlier song, "Abendempfindung." The first case, the later Mozart work, expresses the subject of the incarnation of Jesus Christ, and the earlier composition expresses a general principle which he related to the experience of accepting the reality of the death of his own father. The intended similarities of the manner in which Mozart concludes both compositions, is properly—and intentionally—startling. The point to be considered, is the question of the intent for the existence of both of the two respective compositions; does the performance of that composition actually satisfy that intent? Or, is the performance pretty, but fails to capture the awesomeness of the idea expressed by the kindred intent of both compositions?

In a comparison of those two compositions, Mozart himself provides the means, within the design of composition, for the singers' musical fulfilment of Mozart's intent. Will the singers subject themselves to fulfilling the prescribed mission assigned by the composer, or will the subject of that intent be confined to the mere words spoken as if they were a critic's commentary supplied as a debatable description of the composition, rather than the actuality of the passion embodied in the attempted true performance of the composer's (e.g., Mozart's) intention?

The Classical song-form expressed in use by great composers, affords us the most convenient opportunity for recognizing what the legacy of Johann Sebastian Bach enables the insightful composer from Bach's following to do, and, hopefully, the performers, too.

That accomplishment depends upon a dramatic quality of an implicitly metaphorical principle of Classical irony. If that objective is realized, the musical performance uplifts the performer's and audience's experience to that of a domain of substance, rather than the mere shadows represented by merely ordinary faith in sense-perception.

"What is Hecuba to him, that he should weep for her?"

On this same account, I have often stressed the significance of Albert Einstein's violin bearing on his powers as a scientific discoverer.

Recently, my associates and I have been privileged to extend that sort of example, with much assistance from relevant colleagues, to the case of the family history of Lejeune Dirichlet's marriage to the granddaughter of Moses Mendelssohn, and, thence, to the heart of the wealth of ironies represented by the great body of scientific and musical-artistic genius represented by this association of the giants of the Nineteenth Century poetry, drama, music, and science, through to the time of the close of the lifetime of that century, and of Clara Schumann and Johannes Brahms, too.[13]

There is nothing merely coincidental in such an expressed affinity of great science and great Classical art as those Nineteenth-century circles represent. The creative powers of the scientist are located, essentially, within the domain of the creative realizations of the imagination, as in the domain chosen by the Abraham Kästner who expressed the common modern heritage of Gottfried Leibniz and Johann Sebastian Bach, that domain of the Classical artistic imagination in which crucial scientific discoveries are generated for the en-

---

13. David Shavin, "The Musical Soul of Scientific Creativity: Rebecca Dirichlet's Development of the Complex Domain," **EIR**, June 11, 2010, and Michelle Rasmussen, "Robert and Clara Schumann, and Their Teacher, J.S. Bach," **EIR**, June 18, 2010.

richment of a mundane economic existence.

This function of great Classical musical composition is complemented by that same principle of irony which is specific to Classical prosody. Indeed, the best expositions of physical scientific progress, are provided by appropriately generous use of a mode of use of language which is ordered according to Classical prosody. Lack of such a refined expression leaves an otherwise competent scientific worker seemingly tongue-tied in the effort to present even what had been a competently crafted act of discovery.

These considerations which I have just emphasized, are not merely art; they represent the ante-room of a quality of a science of irony, of true metaphor, an outlook which is urgently needed for the present challenges of a largely scrambled, present world economy.

The Great Pyramind of Giza, near Cairo. "In the history of ancient Egypt," LaRouche writes, "the idea associated with the erection of the Great Pyramid, stands out as a symptom of a cardinal quality of existence in time...."

Method in History

The name of "history," has two contrasted references. One is history as expressed in a chronological order of events; the other, is expressed as the qualitatively superior, internal history of the flow and ebb of those cardinal ideas which generate those changes in physical states, the results of which are expressed in the form of the effective outcome of that which is experienced as merely enumerable chronological history.

For example, in the history of ancient Egypt, the idea associated with the erection of the Great Pyramid, stands out as a symptom of a cardinal quality of existence in time, as does, similarly, the impact of the role of that intellectual giant of Egyptian science, the Platonic Cyrenaican Eratosthenes. Similarly, consider the qualitative difference of the Constitution of the United States, and the effects of that aspect of history, from the course of ordinary events in current world history otherwise.

So, within the history of the United States, there are two opposing cardinal histories, the one being that of the British East India Company's influence on the U.S.A., which is the history of a branch of British imperial history, and the related, but opposing history, the current of our U.S. patriots, which is, essentially, an anti-British history. The latter contrast is shown most clearly in the history, since 1763, of the vicinity of the coastal region of New England from Newburyport to Boston. The history of Salem, Massachusetts from the late Seventeenth Century, with its notorious "witch trials," also has a peculiar ring of the coming British East India Company.

It is not events which dominate history as a process; it is the influences of cardinal ideas which shape events.

Take the case of the current situation in the U.S.A. The U.S. Congress of today, especially the Senate, and especially much of its present Democratic majority, sometimes seems to be virtually a political rats' nest of nearly treasonous follies. However; the "clean out" of the House of Representatives which is already in progress during the present approach to the coming November election, affects the entirety of the present composition of that body, as distinguished from the case for the approximately, only one-third of those to be elected for the Senate.[14] In the meantime, nearly 80% of the eligible U.S. voters, according to a recent poll, showed themselves as in support of an immediate restoration of that Glass-Steagall statute which had been installed

---

14. In the present circumstances, we may anticipate the likelihood of the failure of an elected member of the Senate to be seated.

under President Franklin Roosevelt, in 1933, but repealed, in 1999, that under massive pressure exerted in the form of a brutal swindle carried out under local direction from the British empire's "Wall Street" and virtually treasonous influences of kindred agents of influence inside the U.S.A. That repeal represents a British subversive operation deployed, chiefly, from London, and, also, the heritage of the U.S. branch of the British East India Company embodied, still today, in those Wall Street financier interests, whose efforts have been to make a hapless U.S.A. a virtually captive property of the British empire.

Or, since we are presently on that particular subject, consider the notion of an essentially symbolic value of a currency, or kindred notions of money, as distinct from the processes which are expressed by the production and consumption of actual wealth.

Now, the formation of a popular "mass strike" formation, whose effect is expressed by that nearly 80% of the adult population who oppose the Democratic Party-led majority in the U.S. Senate on the Glass-Steagall issue, typifies the kind of social phenomena-in-process which expresses the weightier role of the history of ideas.

Most important, is the distinction between a mere poll of the opinion of individuals, and the more serious character of a poll of social formations, formations which are to be defined in terms of a body of those persons who define themselves by their common, actively systemic association with categorical ideas. From the latter vantage-point, it is not the mere relative number of persons, as individuals, which shapes history, but, rather, the special quality of relative impact of some, often exceptionally rare individuals, who typify a body of persons motivated by the implicitly revolutionary, virtual social integument of "fighting expressions of notions of principle," as contrasted with a collection of what are merely individual voters otherwise.

This conception, which I have just described, thus far, if in a preliminary, relatively superficial way, can be better understood from a more rigorous standpoint, as follows.

Symbol or Substance?

Consider, in a fresh way, as much as I have written here thus far. Let us now proceed, as I have indicated this intention earlier in this present chapter, to go beyond identifying principles in terms of their describable apparent effects, to consider the matter of considering those same apparent effects as primarily, seemingly self-subsisting expressions of an unseen, but practically efficient reality of existence. It is a matter of locating the actual object which corresponds to the shadow represented for us, customarily, as a sense perception.

The issue, as I had written at some significant length during the preceding year, is that of the actual distinction of shadow (sense-perception) from the real substance which exists beyond sense-perception, a substance which mankind may know best in terms of the experimental proof of existence of those efficient principles which reign in the universe, but are principles which are not known directly through sense-perception as such.

This is pretty much the same thing as the distinction of true universal physical principles, which express directly that which governs our universe, from what are, in truth, the mere shadows of the domain of simply local sense-perceptions.

Think! How should we proceed to design a robot who would simulate some of the general, task-oriented forms of problem-solving functions performed by human individuals? Presume that we are successful in that mission—up to a certain point. That "point" is to be identified as the critical state of affairs in which the robot is sending us what is the increasingly desperately repeated message, one translatable, in principle, as demanding, perhaps desperately: "principle? principle!? …give me the principle which governs this situation!"

That hypothetical (but not really so very hypothetical) case, is the perceived case for an anti-entropic change from the pre-existing repertoire of the previously known closed set of universal principles expressed in an ever-increasing variety of efforts required for controlling the continuing, anti-entropic experience of exploring our universe. Where, then, under those circumstances, is the innermost identity of the scientist and creative Classical artist, alike, to be located, by us?

I suggest, as a first step, that one take time for a thoughtful study based on the prompting of the 1947 edition of William Empson's **Seven Types of Ambiguity**. Empson may not present the answer to the most crucial questions which are implicitly posed in any serious effort to apply his inspiring argument as developed, up to that date, as implicitly stated then and there; but, as I have insisted, repeatedly, to all who would hear, that over the course of subsequent decades, since 1947, if we put the figure of William Empson off our stage for the moment, to bring on the person playing the part of the figure of a useful robot, the latter figure, the robot, does excellent work in posing some of the most relevant and provocative questions which he leaves to be answered by qualified scientists, or a like quality of thinker, still today. Who, then, supplies the answers for questions posed by the frustrated robot of the case I have now presented?

The procedure which I propose to you now, goes as follows.

I have already presented to you, the included notion of an image of man or woman as ordinarily regarded as being like a robot, or like a quality of simulated, human-like form of actual life, in all, but one crucially distinguishing feature. That distinguishing feature is expressed as truly scientific, or kindred creativity, as in Classical art, a figure such as that expressed by Filippo Brunelleschi's discovery of the physical principle of the catenary. The mere existence of such creativity as that, is a feature which is rejected among all followers of the specifically Liberal ideology of Paolo Sarpi and his apostle Galileo. I refer to followers such as René Descartes, such as the authors of the Isaac Newton hoax, and the social philosophy of François Quesnay, Adam Smith, and Jeremy Bentham.[15]

The view of Paolo Sarpi, Galileo, and their followers such as Descartes, Abbé Antonio S. Conti, John Locke, and Adam Smith, is that they deny the knowable existence of any universal principles, substituting a crude, statistical form of reading of pragmatism which may be recognized as philosophical Liberalism. Despite the merely secondary differences between the a-

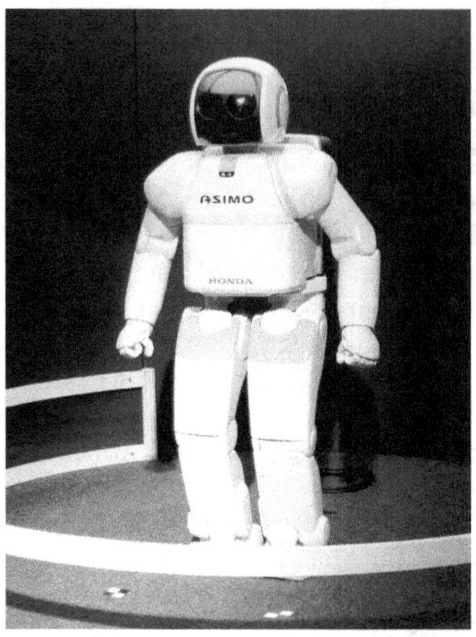

Creative Commons/Gnsin

We can design robots, like Honda's ASIMO, to perform some humanoid tasks, even perhaps some of a problem-solving nature, up to a certain point. But that "point" comes when the robot desperately demands: "Principle?! Give me the principle which governs this situation!"

priorist arguments of the Physiocrats, and the crude plagiarism of entire chunks of the writings of both Quesnay and Turgot by Adam Smith, the viewpoint of all of them was essentially consistent with the principled features of the doctrine of the Liberalism of Paolo Sarpi.[16]

Such virtual "universal robots" as those persons, are clearly not the real human beings who make important discoveries of physical principle. Since we know that we have the kind of creative powers of mind which are capable of generating the discoveries of principle which no virtual robot could supply, we must, like Goethe's three kings, as represented by the Romantic composer Hugo Wolf, toddle on to the next stable, to find the person who can respond to the perplexed robot's question.

Therefore, being human by nature, rather than robots, we must regard ourselves as standing outside the image of mankind which sense-perception as such supplies. Since we are enabled to place our real selves outside the mere sensory figure we mistake ourselves to be; we must view the virtual robot's perplexity as being inherent in being a mere object ("objectively") of our proper intention.

We, the real "we," who are qualified to embody the power of creativity, are not mere objects, but singularities. We are lately convinced that we actually dwell, as singularities, in a domain of cosmic radiation which is inhabited by singularities.

What does that mean?

Once any among us has recognized the nature of human creativity, as Archytas and his friend Plato did, or Nicholas of Cusa, or Gottfried Leibniz, or Friedrich Schiller, or Bernhard Riemann, or any who came to

---

15. Quesnay's work was guided, as to principle, by the transmitted influence of the notorious Venetian mountebank Abbé Antonio S. Conti, who, in concert with his lackey known as Voltaire, launched the anti-Leibniz cult of the post-1715, Eighteenth Century. Quesnay's own social doctrine was premised, by his own account, on the presumption that, since peasant serfs were only a form of cattle, that it was the miraculous powers of the title of the ennobled holder of the rural estate, which were the only source of what should be considered as the lawful profit of labor by society.

16. Adam Smith had been adopted, about the time of the 1763 Peace of Paris, as a spy in the service of Lord Shelburne's newborn empire of Shelburne's British East India Company. Smith's assignment was to spy against the designated targets in both the American English colonies and in France. To this end, Smith insinuated himself into the service of Turgot, thus gaining access to lift large chunks from Turgot's manuscript-in-progress to his own 1776 **The Wealth of Nations**.

walk the same pathway of human reason, we know what a human being can, and must become. The fact that the mere mathematician must regard us as being "merely human," does not strip us of any part of those creative powers which we either can, or could recognize in ourselves. The difference between those who are consciously creative in the degree I have indicated here, and the typical reductionist often found among academic professionals, is that we are prone to think as did such as Gottfried Leibniz and Riemann typify the character of the mind of great discoverers such as themselves.

This, now, brings us to the crucial point to be made in this chapter.

The Secret Self

The immediate outcome of the argument which I have developed in this chapter thus far, is that the discovery of one's own true human nature, requires that the sense of one's human identity be considered in two aspects. The one aspect is that of the experiencing of sense-perception. The other is the view of the experiencing of sense-perception as merely a shadow of reality.

This correction is shown most simply and efficiently by aid of reflections on Johannes Kepler's uniquely original discovery of a universal principle of gravitation as experienced for the case of no less than three or more planetary orbits of our Solar system. This was the discovery which required consideration of the ironical juxtaposition of the faculties of vision and hearing, the one as now associated with the uses of the telescope, the other with the principle of musical harmonics. No single sense could determine the truth; only a juxtaposition of crucially contrasted modes of sense-perception, could lead us to the demonstration of the relativity of the existence of a unique juncture of the mental reading of two contradictory senses, a conjuncture whose uniqueness disclosed the existence of the relevant universal principle.

That case points to a more general consideration. The human mind does not reside within the mere faculty of the human sense-perceptual apparatus. Our senses enjoy the status of being "merely" essential instrumentation required to facilitate the actual powers of the human mind, as distinguished from the sensory function itself.

It should be pointed out, that the distinction of the human being from the animal species, does not rest on that bare fact alone. There is only one distinction of the human mind which defines the uniqueness of the human mind among all other known living species: *the manifest power of the principle located, uniquely, in the human creative imagination.*

According to the dogma of Sarpian Liberalism, as typified by British Liberalism, this power does not exist in the universe of man's power of knowledgeable experience.

Nonetheless, insofar as human existence depends upon the discovery and employment of universal physical principles which are generated into a form of existence by the creative powers specific to the typical human mind, the transmission of the experience of a true discovery of principle, from a person who had lived, to a person who relives that change in perceived reality which is experienced, is the most conspicuous among the factors which distinguish the human species from all known others. Such, and significantly comparable actions are the distinction of the human mind, and of humanity.

The crucial point to be emphasized in that connection, is that the discovery of physical principle, for example, is a physically efficient transmission of power from one generation toward a next. This is typified by the increase of power, per capita, and per square kilometer, of any discovery of universal physical principle. This is the key to defining the principle of personal immortality inherent in the notion of individual human creativity. The potential for such action, by the human individual, is the crucial distinction of man from bestiality.

The practical implication of what is presented in this present chapter, up to this point, is that we must not permit the human individual to be denied access to knowledge of the type which I have outlined in this chapter. For, the fact of the matter is, that the human identity resides not in the fact of sense-perception as such, but in the immortal quality of action expressed by the discovery and transmission of true principles which are relevant to the persistence and progress of the quality and power of the human species and its work.

The import to be emphasized here, is that we must effect the awareness, by the conscious individual, of the distinction of the quality of the nature and relative power of creative ideas, from the products of what is merely the experience of sense-perceptions as such. Thus, we must distance the notion of a true self from those mechanisms which are merely the instruments of coordination of the relevant action of the human individual, as a sovereign, to what lies "outside" the domain of sense-perception as such.

In other words, the typical defect of the individual in society, generally, today, is that the quality of the notion of "I" must be limited to this side of sense-perception, that which stands in opposition to, "outside" of the processes of sense-perception as such. It is within those bounds that the creative faculty is located. Accordingly, the typical intellectual failure in society presently, is the errant attempt to adduce the creative process from the effects of the sense-perceptual process as such. To avoid such blunders responsible for such effects, it is essential to locate the notion of creativity as the power of a notion of mind ("I") which is apart from, but in control of the processes of sense-perception, and the notion of "me."

See one's sensory self as in a mirror, as in the predicament of the Apostle Paul's "glass darkly." The power of creativity is thus assigned to that function of the "soul" and its peculiar conceptions, which is the location of those implicitly immortal, creative powers specific to mankind, rather than the bestiality of the mere senses.

III. The Economy of the Human Mind

As I have emphasized in several pieces published earlier, it is necessary that we approach the tasks of an urgently needed recovery of the U.S.A.'s and other economies, by superseding a commonplace, but shallow-minded use of the term "infrastructure," through imposing the actually relevant terms borrowed from a science of those noëtic principles of the human mind which underlie a science of physical economy, rather than continuing the commonplace, but systemically flawed notion of a merely monetarist economy.

I have illustrated my argument to that effect by the following listing of general stages of civilized European economic development: 1.) maritime economy; next, 2.) inland waterways; next, 3.) transcontinental railway systems; and, next, 4.) "maglev" systems. A relevant kind of alternate ordering, is the distinction of qualities of infrastructure applied to the succession of steps of progress: 1.) wood and charcoal burning, 2.) coal and coke, 3.) petroleum, 4.) natural gas and comparable fuels, 5.) nuclear fission, 6.) thermonuclear fusion, and, 7.) beyond that, such as "matter/anti-matter" power.

Then, suddenly, next, we have, 8.) the perspective of the Moon-Mars development-mission turns up, together with needed development of technologies for human travel in nearby Solar space. Next, 9.) the technologies on which development of habitable stations in relatively near-by Solar space depends.

While such successions in the development of systems of infrastructure continue to be underway, the practice of industry and agriculture may undergo slower rates of qualitative advances in categories of technology than that occurring among the series of developments in infrastructure which I have suggested immediately above. In large part, this difference reflects the fact, that advances in quality, and relative intensity of *energy-flux density*, are actually the drivers of the environment for agriculture, industry, and modes of family, neighborhood life, and urban qualities of organization of community life.

In reviewing the span of the considerations I have just outlined in the opening of this chapter, some points should be listed under the heading of "what should be obvious":

We approach the not-so-distant state of affairs with the warning that in preparing for persons departing Earth for other places in the Solar System, we must recognize the urgency of *either* systems of *artificial gravity, or the functional equivalent*, as an essential prerequisite. Later, somewhere down the line, comes the notion of artificial "planets." With all of this in the sweep of things just suggested thus far, we should introduce the functional conception of distant creation of "artificial planets" as a convenient choice of goal used to convey a sense of the process of development. This is a choice which should be adopted to define the proper choice of scientific meaning for certain future goals. These are included goals which define the proper intention of what we might assign as the meaning of what should be called "the economic function of infrastructure" during present times.

Review the set of cases just presented in a slightly different set of terms of reference.

The first major advance beyond the scope of maritime forms of physical-economic systems within European colonization, was indicated by the primarily military function of Roman roads and aqueducts. However, the development of European inland waterways, systems of rivers, and canals, under Charlemagne, was crucial economically. Later, as I have emphasized in other locations, the development of transcontinental railway systems in the U.S.A. was the great advance which, by being spread in post-1875 Germany and Russia, constituted a fundamental threat to the maritime supremacy of the British Empire, such that, from the time of the British empire's accomplishing the ouster of Germany's Chancellor Bismarck in 1890, onward, the British empire launched a cumulative use of international wars, following the Anglo-Japan alliance against China, Korea, and Russia, of the 1895-1941 period, and Japan's 1940-1945 break with Britain itself.

In the beginning of the 1920s, Britain and Japan had led in a plot to develop Japan's navy for that intended attack on Pearl Harbor which Japan actually launched in December 1941, an attack since officially dated by the U.S.A. to December 7, 1941. The Churchill launching of what was to become dated as the 1946-1989 so-called "Cold War" against Russia, was an expression of the continued British imperialist policy of the 1890-1989 interval. Similarly, the November 22, 1963 assassination of President John F. Kennedy, would soon end U.S. refusal to be drawn into that prolonged U.S. war in Indo-China which, chiefly, was intended, successfully, to ruin the economy of the U.S.A.

As I have emphasized in earlier publications, the function of war in European history since the Peloponnesian War, has been, often, as since Britain's orchestration of the 1756-1763 so-called "Seven Years War" in Europe, and like the similar British intention behind the Napoleonic wars within continental Europe, to prompt Britain's rivals to destroy themselves for the sake of the greater glory of Britain's empire. Similarly, the cutting back of the U.S. transcontinental railway system, for the sake of the automobile traffic, since the close of World War II, has been a systemic weakening of the net productivity of the U.S. economy, both by direct means, and also by changes in the organization of urban society within U.S. territory. The same thing was among the measures used by the British empire in the closing weeks of 1989, to launch the destruction of the national economy of a reunited Germany.[17]

____

17. As, that empire has been expressed by the post-February 1968 completion of Prime Minister Harold Wilson's launching of the Autumn 1967 revaluation of the British pound, the consequent February 1968 revaluation of the U.S. dollar, and subsequently overlapping 1971 events of the shutting down of the U.S.-launched fixed-exchange-rate system, and the related fact of Lord Jacob Rothschild's launching of the British empire's Inter-Alpha Group. Also, the wrecking of the U.S. economy by David Rockefeller's Trilateral Commission under the U.S. government of President Jimmy Carter and the new J.P. Morgan operations openly launched during the period of the first Reagan Administration, including the keystone wrecking roles against the U.S. dollar played by Alan Greenspan during, and since the decade of the 1980s.

Accordingly, we must think of basic economic infrastructure in terms of the concept of a direction of change under conditions of evolving national economic systems of organized, comprehensive development of national and international territory, that done to such effect that such infrastructural development defines the principal parameter of national economic growth and productivity. It will be much later in the "space age," that needed policy will ultimately reach speculation on man's use of "artificial planets."

Consider this view of the economy of infrastructure from the standpoint of the fact that we had already, implicitly, entered the age of human interplanetary exploration during the 1950s. The 1920s through 1940s development of rocket systems, had been begun with the intention of man's landing on the Moon. Even the development of military rocket-systems based on the German pioneering with this technology during the period of the Hitler regime, was, in fact, a side-trip relative to what had been initially intended to be merely a by-product of the manned Moon-Landing perspective of the pre-Hitler-regime period.

It is not necessary, nor desirable, to burden this present report, with anything more respecting space travel than essential features of the subject assigned to this present chapter's contributions to the subject of the needed economic development of humanity's entry into control over nearby space. It is sufficient to focus on the space-mission as viewed by the late Krafft Ehricke's notions of industrialization of the Moon as preparation for the Mars mission. It were sufficient to say, that the very continued existence of mankind needs options for the contingency of threats to life on Earth which may be matters of reasonable concern several generations down the way. Making it to Mars would be the token success which strongly suggests that mankind can succeed in much more awesome choices of goals.

However, we must qualify our thinking about such matters, by noting that we must eventually come around to focus on some actually galactic goals; we must be prompted to believe that we will almost certainly require a period of some few centuries, or more, to reach some actually galactic goals. Hence, we do not have an indefinite amount of time to waste on catering to U.S. President Barack Obama's Nero-like foolishness.

Among what is already clear for a time several generations just ahead, is that a journey to Mars which would require several, or more hundred days journey, is not an acceptable prospect for human travelers. Instruments, including robots, are already standard types of

Krafft Ehricke's Vision

The late Krafft Ehricke (1917-84), space scientist and passionate advocate for space exploration, summarized his philosophy of astronautics in three laws (1957):

First Law. Nobody and nothing under the natural laws of this universe impose any limitations on man except man himself. Second Law. Not only the Earth, but the entire Solar System, and as much of the universe as he can reach under the laws of nature, are man's rightful field of activity. Third Law. By expanding through the universe, man fulfills his destiny as an element of life, endowed with the power of reason and the wisdom of the moral law within himself.

The first law is astronautics' challenge to man to write his declaration of independence from *a priori* thinking, from uncritically accepted conditions, in other words, from a past and principally different pre-technological world clinging to him. This can be done. The Declaration of Independence and the Constitution of this country prove it.

—Cited in Marsha Freeman, *How We Got to the Moon: The Story of the German Space Pioneers* (Washington, D.C., 21st Century Science Associates, 1993), p. 297.

Krafft Ehricke with a model of an orbital hospital.

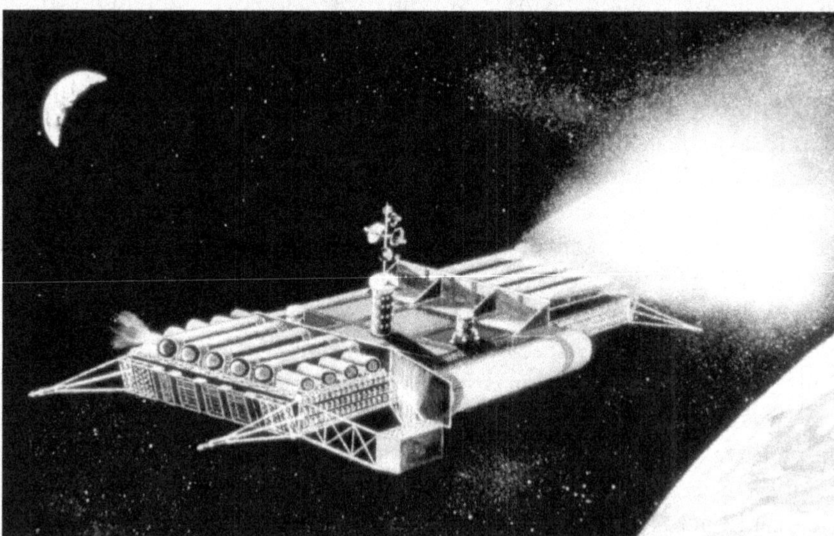

Painting of a nuclear freighter for industrialization of the Moon, by Krafft Ehricke.

technologies, but the safe transport of human life can not be compared with hauling freight, and until we can bring relevant humans to the surface of Mars through the advantages of accelerated/decelerated trajectories, there are sundry monstrous impediments to certain kinds of scientific progress needed for coming to understand that planet to the degree needed for defining and realizing what must become our medium to long range intentions for the extra-terrestrial destiny of mankind within nearby Solar space.

So, accelerated transport of human crew and passengers to Mars orbit, soon becomes a cardinal feature of mankind's dealing with the perils and opportunities for those accomplishments in nearby space which will become essential for those of us staying behind for our related duties here. Accelerated/decelerated trajectories are essential.

Cosmic Radiation

Even before a likely manned landing on Mars, which may require preparations during several generations to come,[18] we must come to grips with the reality, that there is "no empty space" out there. Contrary to what might

---

18. As a result of the destruction and the retrogression of the economies and cultures of the trans-Atlantic regions since 1968, the ability to fulfill manned missions within nearby space has been set back by several generations since the catastrophic degree of cultural setbacks since the early 1980s. Two generations will be needed to bring the trans-Atlantic economies, and potential labor-forces back to the quality of competence which was still recoverable during the early part of the 1980s.

be wrongly considered to be some "empty space" between the orbits of Earth and Mars, the illusion of the existence of "empty space," is to be recognized as what might be considered as the result of a "planning failure" in the design of humanity's sense-organs.

What is called "space" is jammed-full of a mass of varieties of cosmic radiation. Thus, one of the tasks to be tackled beginning the very near future, is a certain degree of reorganization of the so-called "periodic table" of physical chemistry, to reflect the implications of a space jammed full of cosmic radiation assorted into sundry sorts of variously "hard" and "soft" radiation flowing from and to assorted potential targets. My relevant associates and their collaborators have, so far, only "scratched the surface" of this complex.

This challenge has been expressed by the celebrated example of particle-wave paradoxes of the celebrated experiments of de Broglie and those who contributed to the matter of the broader implications of his discovery.[19] The relevant evidence presents us the strong suggestion that the reading of the periodic table must be restated in terms of these considerations of "wave functions" in the domain of cosmic radiation, as such a view is typified by Academician V.I. Vernadsky's partition of physical space-time among the abiotic, the biosphere, and the noösphere.

So, the most attractive approach to this subject as a whole, should turn our attention to the work of the associates of the Riemannian physical chemist, Soviet Academician V.I. Vernadsky and his contemporary collaborators. The leading issues on this account reported to me, refer to the impact on the implications of an updated physical chemistry for understanding that exotic physical chemistry of those living processes which lie within the extended domain of the periodic table.

Matters already reported on this account, already tend to go as far as suggesting, that instead of simply continuing the development of the "periodic table," we must emphasize "the periodic table of the chemistry of living processes within the domain of cosmic radiation," and locate the related aspects of specifically human creativity as a category to be considered in related terms.

I shall be more emphatic, as follows.

Return your attention to the general conclusion of the preceding chapter of this report: the distinction be-

There is no "empty space" out there: "What is called "space' is jammed-full of a mass of varieties of cosmic radiation." Shown is the Eagle Nebula (M16).

tween the notion of the defective notion of human ontology which is premised upon deductions from sense-perception, as against an ontology premised upon the exemplary implications of the evidence, as that is to be found in Kepler's unique solution for the concept of general gravitation. The way in which we define man and human behavior experimentally, determines the way in which we must assess the experimental evidence represented by attempts at experimental interpretation of the universe we inhabit. I am treating my subject-matter of this present chapter, from the standpoint which I have already emphasized in my concluding view of the matter expressed within the preceding chapter.

Considering all just said, up to this point of the present chapter, return now to a comparison of the implied content of both the preceding chapter, and what I have written thus far in this present chapter. I return to further treatment of the subject of "The Secret Self."

'As in a Mirror, Darkly'

Travel to the domain of the imagination. Award to the member of our human species the possibility, that, in some fashion we can recognize that our identity as personalities resides in what we name, but usually do not actually understand rightly, as "a spiritual domain."

---

19. These subject-matters are the province of relevant associates of mine, who have more to say on these matters on appropriate occasions and future times.

Thus, we do know that *that identity itself actually exists as an efficient entity, and that it employs the sensory apparatus as a tool of what we recognize as our conscious existence as living persons.*

On reflection, however, we should recognize that this quality of a sovereign entity, a kind of "higher personality," is our true self. We should be enabled to recognize this fact in the higher arts of the imagination, as in that scientific imagination which expresses that Classical artistic imagination, which William Empson yearned to identify as if seen out of the corner of his mind's eye. It is the imagination of John Keats' **Ode on a Grecian Urn**, and of the concluding paragraph of Percy Bysshe Shelley's **A Defence of Poetry**.

It is also the principle of drama which Shakespeare puts on stage, in those cases in which the director and actors of a performance were capable of recognizing the rarely understood principle involved, even from among the putative experts in such matters today. Such a drama, that of ancient Greek Classical drama, such as that of Aeschylus' **Prometheus Bound**, is properly performed from behind the masks, or to kindred effect, by a director and actors who recognize that the personality on stage has no equivalence to the performer who appears before the curtain after the curtain is finally run down for that occasion. The play which is to be performed, as from behind the mask, in the imagination of the audience, and the actors and setting, must be that which presently exist only in the imagination, at whatever location in past or (possibly) the past, present, or future time and place to which the imagination of the author and the company have taken the audience.

The same eeriness of that artfully staged reality, is also specific to Shelley's **A Defence of Poetry**. That is the mysterious, invisible, but efficient potency which moves a certain mass of people even contrary to their personal willful inclination, as Shelley identifies this, or the "mass strike," as Rosa Luxemburg identified what is actually Shelley's principle of history as an actually historical phenomenon. The human individual is not contained within his, or her skin; there are radiant influences which express, or invade the willful intent of the individual member of society, members which sometimes gather as subjects of some common principle which moves them. Ontologically, that aspect of the influence variously radiated by, or upon the individual, is of the same inclusive species as the act of a valid discovery of scientific principle. Classical artistic functions of creative insight, and the discovery of scientific principle, are a common ground in such matters as these. Such are the proper forces which bind together the masterful playwright's composition of the life-like drama presented as if on the Classical stage of an Aeschylus, Shakespeare, Lessing, or Schiller.

To supply the relevant, necessary restatement of the point which I have just made here, consider the following illustration.

Consider a set of incarnate players on the stage of what passes among the innocent for a sensible reality and its associated passions. In such a fashion as that, compare yourself as the sensible mortal carcass which you inhabit, to the real self for whom all sensibility is composed of what are mere objects on which the real self is sometimes enabled to impose a willful impulse.

Consider the case, in which that personal real self, discovers an insight into the significance of the events presented by sense-perception, proceeding as if those events of sense-perception were shadows cast upon perceptions by the relevant realities. In that state of affairs, the real self wishes to shout a warning to his or her incarnate self; let it be the case, that in some fashion, that warning is received by the puppet, the sense-perceptible aspect of himself, or herself, as like an ominous whisper heard as an eerie intimation from a higher, metaphysical domain.

How might we explain this?

Look at the array of the individual person's sense-experiences. The real self, which has no sensory organs in itself, contemplates the images presented to it by the senses. The real self now judges the behavior of what he, or she regards as the shadows of that relatively puppet-like sense-behavior attributed to the perceived stage. The real self now judges the conduct and intentions of the figure within the domain of sense-perceptions, and as the phenomena of the "mass strike" reflect this, such that the affected portion of the population will be moved to act accordingly, so as to produce the effects perceived as from within the domain of sense-perceptible experiences.

Mass phenomena, such as the "mass strike" phenomenon identified by Rosa Luxemburg, demonstrate the efficiency of what Shelley described in the concluding paragraphs of his **A Defence of Poetry**. Creative scientific insights by the individual, or a small circle of individuals, have the same quality of significance. Such are the valid qualities of insight into what controls the domain of hands and feet when such insight has intervened upon the domain of the puppets of sense-certainties.

It is to the degree that the better-developed Classical artist or scientist, such as Johannes Kepler, is at peace with the fact of the distinction of the higher powers of his or her inner person, that the power of human creativity is promoted, as in the instance of Albert Einstein's insight into the implication of Kepler's discovery, or Mozart's intention in his **Ave Verum Corpus**, in the form of a self-consciousness of this creativity. Such persons, so matured, have entered a state of mind in which they have acquired the ability to know themselves as something better than in the likeness of more or less civilized beasts.

Such are the hallmarks of true human creativity.

This is the ontological quality of creativity which man must take into exploration in nearby and more distant space. Such are the powers of insight which must be permitted to drive the upward quality of development of the quality of human existence, either on Earth, or in space.

Human creativity, so conceived, is the unique quality of human creativity, which ultimately sets mankind apart from the apes and worms alike.

IV. The Two-Plus "Realities"

Now, so far in this present report, we have indicated two realities. First, there is the apparent reality of sense-certainties. This is the merely apparent reality which is to be presumed as such, when considered from the standpoint of both crude sense-perception (e.g., materialism) and, also, that empiricism of the followers of Paolo Sarpi for which there are no actual universal physical principles, but only, as Adam Smith wrote in his **Theory of the Moral Sentiments**, statistical sense-uncertainties. Second, we have the principal other reality, that of experimentally validated, universal physical principles. The question so posed for the victim, such as the typical victim of the currently prevalent, trans-Atlantic, and currently ruinous practice of finance and accounting, is, apparently: "Which is true?"

The reply to that question is, that, since universal physical principles, otherwise identified as experimentally demonstrated universal physical laws, actually exert control over the destiny of the subject-matters of sense-perceptions, must we not draw the obvious conclusions from that fact?

Put the point in another way. Take the particular case of the notion of the catenary, or the related notion of Gottfried Leibniz's principle of universal, physical least action. Or, take the general case of Riemannian physical geometry, as opposed to Euclidean or related kinds of nominalist geometries. Look at this difference in terms of the customary efforts to distinguish the "physical" from the currently "sentimental." Which among such mutually contentious distinctions, wins out in the end?

Or, is it not the case, that we employ ordinary sense-certainty for the reading of one kind of an empirically Leibnizian view of a situation, and the higher form, that of discovered universal physical principles, for the other. Insofar as we do not confuse the proper employment for the one case and the proper employment of the other, there is no problem, excepting the need to distinguish statements which should be recognized as based on the phenomena of sense-certainty, from those based on the underlying crucial-experimental authority of the discovery of universal physical principles, the latter as in the example of the discovery of gravitation by Kepler, in his **Harmonies**, as this has been assessed by Albert Einstein.

It happens, that when we go outside the limits of customary sense-perception, into what is for us the extremely large, or the extremely small, we must, as Bernhard Riemann warned us that we must: we must, then, recognize that we have passed out of the range of limitations within which sense-certainty has its conditional authority.[20] Outside the ranges of those limitations, it is the ostensibly "spiritually physical," which must prevail as being the reality with which we must reckon.

At precisely this point in this report, we should be impelled to return to emphasize Leibniz's notion of *dynamics,* in such a fashion as that which should be associated with such references as Shelley's concluding argument in his **A Defence of Poetry**. This is of particular significance at the present moment of current world history, when the entirety of the economy of the planet is poised at the verge of being plunged into an extremely prolonged dark age of the world's presently reigning, contemporary follies.

This is also the range, in the relatively very large, and the relatively very small, the range in which such experimental distinctions as the "living" and the "cognitive" must prevail. By "cognitive," we must also always intend to include the systemic quality of "creative."

It is precisely the case, that, amid those consider-

---

20. Bernhard Riemann, **Über die Hypothesen, welche der Geometrie zu Grunde liegen**: "III, Anwendung auf den Raum." Bernhard Riemann's gesammelte Mathematische Werke (Heinrich Weber, ed.) 1902; pp. 283-286.

ations, that the concept of "mind" is to be located as a universal principle. It is under the topic of "mind," that the significance of both "sense-certainty" and universal principles, is subsumed. Therefore, when we are dealing with the need to define the universal physical principle by which the actual principles of economy are situated, we must apply strict definitions: human creativity, on which the very existence of the notions of real economy depends, must be recognized as the study of the effects of relevant, mutually contradicting classes of phenomena, as these are determined within that domain of those universal physical principles which are located essentially in the truly Classical-artistic domain of the creative powers of the individual human mind, the domain of true human creativity, the domain of the great Classical dramatist's work of such as Aeschylus and Plato, the true domain of the essential ironies of human knowing.

So, as in the instance of Johannes Kepler's discovery of the principle of universal gravitation, and as Albert Einstein defined Kepler's universe as existing in a current state of being both *finite and yet unbounded*, it is through such paradoxes, that knowledge of truth is gained and imparted. *The truest of known truth is always expressed as metaphor, as in the form of "two, plus, 'realities'."*

Leibniz's 'Infinitesimal'

The proper use of the term "Modern European history" has two distinct meanings, both of which are factually truthful, if ironically so. The lesser meaning is expressed by the term "renaissance:" as a rebirth of civilization from a preceding, prolonged "new dark age." The still higher meaning of "renaissance" for this case, is that supplied to modern European civilization by Nicholas of Cusa. His achievement on this account was set into actual motion by, chiefly, two writings.

The first was his definition of the foundation of the principle of the modern sovereign nation-state: **Concordancia Catholica** (A.D. 1433).[21] The second was his definition of modern science: **De Docta Ignorantia** (A.D. 1440). There was more to follow those writings, but those two expressed that intention which was to come to include all of the elementary foundations of a competent notion of modern European physical science; these two writings express the foundations upon which the entirety of Cusa's subsequent work depended.

All among the foundations of competent modern European science had been, and remain as chiefly reflections of the influences transmitted from the faction represented by Plato, as that and related knowledge has been delivered to us from a period dating through approximately the death of Eratosthenes, and also Cusa's immediate followers. This was delivered as some of this knowledge had been brought to modern Florence, chiefly, as by Cosimo de' Medici and Cusa, from libraries within an already dying Grecian remnant of Byzantium. Cusa's presentation of his own rediscovery of the ancient Christian principle of the *Filioque*, at Florence, that during the time of his role within that Ecumenical Council, is an example of the significance of his relevant scholarship.

The true mainstream of the development of modern European science, as this took shape in the context of the role of the statecraft of Florence's scholarly Cosimo de' Medici, and also the influence of Florence's Filippo Brunelleschi, has been subsequently centered, to the present time, from the impact of Cusa's seminal **De Docta Ignorantia**, as continued through such associates and followers as Luca Pacioli, Luca's intellectual heir Leonardo da Vinci, and the powerful influence of Leonardo's role on the circles in which Johannes Kepler shaped his own contributions to an upward turn in competent science; that is the Kepler from whose work came the most crucial features of Gottfried Leibniz's emergence in the role of the leading mathematical physicist of his own time.

Thus, it was chiefly the impact of Cusa, beginning with his seminal **De Docta Ignorantia**, which has defined the renewed basis for the efficient role of actual physical-scientific progress in modern European economy and culture, and thus defined what has become the leading feature of economic progress in modern society. To reach a competent insight into the underlying motives of modern scientific progress, we must understand the role of the origin of Leibniz's crucial contribution to modern mathematical physical science and to Europe's currents and periods of physical-economic progress, contributions which take their roots in **De Docta Ignorantia**. Here lies the crucial significance of Leibniz's uniquely original discovery of the role of the infinitesimal calculus. That role is to be properly under-

---

21. Although **Concordancia Catholica** had addressed a crisis of organization within the Catholic church at that time, it also had a crucial part in defining the notion of the modern European nation-state republic. The way in which the matter of Jeanne d'Arc's judicial murder was brought to the attention of the Council is notable, as also reflected in the establishment of France under Louis XI, as also England under Henry VII.

stood not as merely a formal-mathematical principle, but, rather, in its true nature as a physical principle, as the point was illustrated by Cusa's **De Ludo Globi**.[22]

That is a creative physical principle expressed by the so-called "infinitesimal," whose discovery, by Leibniz, is rooted directly, and essentially, in Johannes Kepler's discovery of the principle of universal gravitation, as presented in Kepler's **Harmonies**.[23]

Then, from the modern physical science rallied by Leibniz, came that great jewel of modern history known as that modern European notion of the sovereign nation-state economy, a notion launched from within modern Europe, but which is best expressed by the notion of the U.S.A.'s constitutional form of modern European culture's nation-state republic.

The Science of the Nation-State Economy

The birth of the United States as a nation-state, as properly dated, chiefly, from the work of the Seventeenth Century under the charter of the Massachusetts Bay colony, is the crucial development in practice which is, so far, the best approximation of the political role which must express the principled role of the progress of modern physical science in the domain of political-economy.

Such a concept must be traced chiefly to the inspiration which Cardinal Nicholas of Cusa and his close associates performed, as typified by Cusa's proposal that civilization could not achieve its goals in Europe, except as a consequence of seeking opportunities across the oceans, a consequence which could not be secured under the conditions of persisting decadence within Europe itself during the then apparent future.

It was the knowledge of this policy which had been uttered by a then-deceased Nicholas of Cusa, which explicitly informed and inspired a Christopher Columbus who, by A.D. 1480, had already adopted Cusa's policy as the mission of an expedition across the Atlantic to the specific region of the coast of a trans-Atlantic continent. It was from the still-living associates of Cusa, that Columbus was informed of the likely location of the world-map of his destination in what proved to be what we now know as the Americas.[24]

The unfortunate features of the outcome of Columbus's successful discovery in 1492, then, and later, lay both in the fact that Spain and Portugal were coming under the reign of the Habsburg empire, and that the controlling influence over the Habsburg dynasty was the Venetian monetarist interest, one akin, as precedent, to the British imperial interest associated with the 1971 founding of Lord Jacob Rothschild's creation, the Inter-Alpha financial interest dominating much of Europe and the Americas today. The ill-fated aspects of Columbus' achievement, were the product of the fact that the Habsburg interest, then under Venetian domination, had just launched that internecine, religious, international warfare which dominated the 1492-1648 interval.[25]

Thus, the preponderance of prevalent failures of the modern form of civilized development in the regions of the Americas until 1620, was a by-product of the Habsburg interest's grip on the destiny of the region of the Americas under Habsburg control. The developmental problems of the large portion of the nations of the Habsburg-flavored portions of the Catholic community in Europe, are a reflection of this 1492-1648 aspect of a Venetian control which lingers, often in Anglo-Dutch Liberal cloaking, up through the present day.

The working point I am emphasizing by those immediately preceding references of this present chapter, is that the period of the successful development of the Massachusetts Bay settlement, combined with the Eighteenth-century resurgence of that legacy, as has been identified by Graham Lowry's **How the Nation Was Won**, was the success of the establishment of the U.S. Federal Constitution, as contrasted with the relative failures by both the northern and the southern cultures in Europe, so to be seen when their cultures have

---

22. A game, designed by Cusa, contrary to von Neumann and Morgenstern, which I had the good fortune to demonstrate in play, in a relevant setting within the cloister at Bernkastel-Kues.

23. Kepler bequeathed two challenges to "future mathematicians." The first, was the discovery of the infinitesimal calculus, which was accomplished, chiefly, by Leibniz; the second, was the development of that concept of elliptical functions which came to be associated with contemporaries of Carl F. Gauss.

24. As in other relevant cases from that same antiquity, the resources employed by Christopher Columbus' advisors from among the collaborators of Cusa, depended crucially upon Eratosthenes' much earlier, experimental measurement of a fair estimate of the size of the planet Earth, also, of the arc from Alexandria to Rome. The mentality of both Archytas, who solved the duplication of the cube, and Archytas' associate Plato are highly relevant for situating the products of the genius of the Cyrenaican Eratosthenes.

25. For example, it was that same Venice which orchestrated Venice's division of Europe into the continuing warfare of that 1492-1648 interval, through the direct Venetian control over the butcher known as England's errant King Henry VIII, leading into what was to become the later development of what became the rabidly reductionist mode of the Anglo-Dutch Liberal imperialism dominating the world today.

been seen as expressed in settings which were alien to the process which had led to the contrasting formation and achievements of the U.S.A.

Notably, from 1620 to the present period of crisis, the development of what became the continental U.S.A., over the interval 1620-Sept. 14, 1901,[26] was, predominantly the expression of a European culture as expressed by developments within European nationalities. The difference was the United States' large degree of freedom from the kind of oligarchical grip which persisted as the reigning political and social systems of Europe. The European immigrants into the U.S.A. soon acquired the political culture typical of the North American. The most notable of the distinguishing features of the change of location of the typical immigrant transported from Europe into the U.S. cultural setting, was freedom from the residual social trappings of European oligarchical hegemonies.

Similarly, the Lafayette who was a successful hero inside North America, lost something crucial from that quality of performance when he returned to his place in the setting of the oligarchical relics still hegemonic in Europe, as this fact was shown in the Summer of 1789 and in the campaign of 1830. Such phenomena as this difference in what may be fairly identified as "a mass effect," is identified by the closing paragraphs of Shelley's **A Defence of Poetry**, an effect which belongs to the domain emphasized in the concluding paragraphs of his work. Our Federal Constitution defines precisely that distinction.

V. Law: Science Versus Custom

Looking at the physical economy as expressed on that surface of things where the shadow cast by reality

is met, a physical economy exhibits the following, included characteristics.

In the trans-Atlantic tradition so far, we encounter several types of often muddled qualities of law expressed on the visible surface of the economic process. It may appear curious to some, that I should propose, here, that we should recognize that that superior principle of universal law which must be adopted by and among nations, lies within that specific notion of a true principle governing the prescribed role of man and woman in the universe, which is the notion expressed in the opening chapter of **The Book of Genesis.**

Such were the essential distinctions shared under the U.S.A.'s Declaration of Independence, and under the Federal Constitution of the remaining lifetimes of President George Washington and Secretary of the Treasury Alexander Hamilton, as their commitment was echoed, later, under Presidents James Monroe and John Quincy Adams.[27]

In reporting those facts of the First Chapter of Genesis, I must therefore caution the reader, for similar reasons, that the quality of the first chapter of **Genesis** by stating that must not be confused with that of certain other chapters of the same book: the evidence is, that certain later chapters were clearly crafted by the syncretist doings of those perfidious creatures such as the purveyors of the Babylonian-sponsored "Adam and Eve" fable, who dumped large chunks of what were well-known, hideous sorts of both Mesopotamian, and other nonsense inserted into the editing of the revised texts of the captive Hebrew scholars.[28]

Similarly, much of what passes for sanctimonious concoctions in law in the U.S.A. or Europe today, has

---

26. The assassination of the U.S. patriot and President McKinley, by an assassin imported from Europe for this purpose, on Sept. 1, 1901, brought the Vice-President Theodore Roosevelt, the nephew and protégé of the former head of the Confederacy's intelligence service, into the Presidency: an ironical by-product of the post-1876 Hayes-Tilden controversy of that year's Presidential election, a habit of attempted reconciliation between patriots and former Confederates. The replacement of a patriot McKinley by Theodore Roosevelt, was a reversal of policy which caused World War I by the effect of putting a British-imperialism toady Theodore Roosevelt into the Presidency. This change was clarified at Portsmouth, New Hampshire, in Theodore Roosevelt's "negotiated settlement," in favor of Britain's ally Japan against Russia. It was not until the election of Franklin Roosevelt, that the Abraham Lincoln legacy of patriotism was re-established.

27. Jefferson had been a terrible President in the main. Madison had shown the effects of life under a wife, "Dolly," who, as Tony Chaitkin has reported, had been a selection arranged through the flagrant traitor and founder of the London-steered Bank of Manhattan, Aaron Burr. During that period and later, Aaron Burr had been a controlled asset of the Lord Palmerston-appointed Jeremy Bentham then heading the secret intelligence service of the Palmerston-created British Foreign Office, the same Bentham who had supervised the orchestration of what became the Jacobin Terror, and, thus, the subsequent selection of that British asset known as Napoleon Bonaparte, who drowned all continental Europe in his own re-enactment of the Seven Years War, in his folly of his bleeding of continental Europe, through wars of rapine and looting, which reduced continental Europe to a state of ruin of the nations of continental Europe through the time of Waterloo and the consequent London-Habsburg Vienna pact. Britain reigned through such aid from Napoleon.

28. Some may protest against this correction, but the urgent quality of the fact of the matter presently, demands that, this time, we get the actual Mosaic legacy right, free of Babylonian obscenities.

been, similarly, infested with the miserable Adam Smith's doctrine, especially since the death of President Franklin Roosevelt, except for the fact that the constitutional legacy of the U.S.A. constitutional law, as tattered, mutilated, and exploited as it has become, is not only better than most every other national political culture considered, those of Europe notably, but could be repaired, according to its original intention under a suitable Presidential administration.

Accordingly, much of what is dumped upon us as doctrine, in the U.S.A. today, does not fully express, even often violates, the systemic notions of law expressed by both the U.S. Declaration of Independence and original U.S. Federal Constitution. Thus, we suffer presently from massive corruptions of our law, corruptions effected through the hereditary influence of our chief original and continuing foe, the British empire of Lord Shelburne et al., as was imposed through those agents of the British East India Company.

There has been, for example, the corrupting role of such as the British agent, and U.S. traitor-in-fact Aaron Burr, the Burr who founded that Bank of Manhattan, which was launched, explicitly, on behalf of the British East India Company, as by Jeremy Bentham's British Foreign Office's imperial, Wall Street interest. Burr's influence was later shown by the creation of Burr's onetime accomplice Andrew Jackson, the President Jackson who terminated the U.S. National Bank, an action which was taken by Jackson at that time, as would be done later, by J.P. Morgan interests of such as Morgan executive Alan Greenspan, already beginning 1984, against the Glass-Steagall law, for the same, treasonous purpose of plunging the U.S. economy now, as into Martin van Buren's "Panic" of 1837, the latter a swindle which had been introduced through van Buren's Wall Street puppet, President Andrew Jackson, then.

What I am now presenting on that account, in this chapter, is to be carefully considered hereafter, as the outline of a much needed, much overdue improvement in U.S. conception of constitutional law on this account. What I am doing to that end, as I do in this present chapter, is to trace the genesis of our republic from the seed of the mission of such as the founders of the Massachusetts Bay colony under its original charter, and from the circles of Benjamin Franklin and such among his associates as Treasury Secretary Alexander Hamilton, Secretary of State and President John Quincy Adams, and, later, Abraham Lincoln, and President Franklin Roosevelt still later.

The issue is not commitment to consistency with relevant precedent, as if in the original intent of a contract; the issue is defining and defending a principle of government on which the continued existence of civilization depends today and into the future of centuries to come. This requires the elimination of those precedents which have misled the U.S.A. into the follies which have chiefly dominated U.S. policy-making, at increasing rates during most of the Presidencies over the course of the period since the death of President Franklin Roosevelt. Essentially we must rid the nation's practice from the corrupting effects of European monetarist influences, during most of the times since, most notably, the retirement of Presidents such as George Washington, John Quincy Adams, Abraham Lincoln, William McKinley, Franklin Roosevelt, and John F. Kennedy.[29]

My chief contribution to our nation's present hope of its own future now, is typified by my determination to break us free of the grip of monetarism, doing so by taking a rather large, but now urgently needed step, which is both a return to, and the launching of urgently needed measures for progress over the course of coming generations, progress which can not be realized without looking beyond those foundations which are consistent with, but also necessary for our future, foundations to be discovered in the foundations which Franklin Roosevelt had laid.

That is what is being done now by those intended actions of mine which are designed to free us from slavery to those economic relics of Venetian and British practices of a usury which have gained a ruinous form of control over us, through an action which had been accomplished through aid of the assassination of that President John F. Kennedy who had been an impediment to implementation of a British-dictated Indo-China war policy. This subversion by the British and allied adversaries of our republic, has been a subversion which has been typified by the errors of those later Pres-

---

29. The promising aspects of the William Clinton administration were that it delayed much of the damage which would have been done under a second administration of George H.W. Bush, and did essay the effort to deal with the 1998 chain-reaction collapse of the Russian bond speculations, but such achievements were offset by the baggage of Al Gore's Vice-Presidency, and the lingering threat of the impeachment attempted by Wall Street and London. Specifically, when I had pushed, in 1996, for the Clinton administration's opening up cooperation with leading Russian figures, the pressures which Gore imposed on President Clinton's winning a second term were a heavy threat to any attempted rational development in U.S.A.-Russia reforms in economic relations.

idents who proved to be accomplices of the schemes of our British imperial adversaries-in-fact: Presidents such as, most emphatically, Richard Nixon, Jimmy Carter, two George Bushes, and, now, British imperialism's U.S. puppet-President Barack Obama.

The appropriateness of such concerns is sufficiently well defined by facts on the common surface of history and physical science.

Despite the fact that such considerations define my intentions set forth here, those which have been my intention in this publication from the outset here, are intentions which could not have been presented in a politically effective service of my intention, except through emphasis on those topics of a physical science of economy which I have presented in the preceding chapters. The significance of these preceding chapters, on this just stated account, is a matter which goes to the heart of the notion of a science of natural law, a notion of a body of "natural law" premised upon those absolute distinctions of true human nature, the which I have pointed out in those preceding chapters, and which pertain most directly, and most emphatically, to the creative powers which are unique to humanity among all presently known living species.[30]

The repetitions of a systematic destruction of modern civilization, since such evil events as the attempted overturn of the intention of both the modern European Renaissance and the 1648 Treaty of Westphalia. In those recurring attempts at overturning that legacy of that Renaissance, now especially since the momentous consequences of the deaths of U.S. Presidents Franklin D. Roosevelt and John F. Kennedy, could be traced, as a matter of principle, certain diseased, millennial influences in European civilization which correspond to the prophetic warnings in Aeschylus' **Prometheus Trilogy**, as I emphasize that historical fact in the course of this present chapter.

I define the essentials of the needed reform in the following listing of the relevant principles which underlie a competent statement of the physical principles of a sound economy.

---

30. I would argue, that when we take into account the implications of what I have written on the relationships between man's sense-perceptual shadow and inner reality, in preceding chapters here, the existence of what might appear to be forms with a quality of intelligence specific to mankind, but in a different form of existence, can not be excluded as "other expressions" of a species of creative being under other planetary conditions. This is implicit in the fact of the universality of life as a principle of the domain of universal cosmic radiation.

Science & Political-Economy

Therefore, let us now restate the case for the design of an economy on our Earth in the form of a concise summary of those arguments which are to be recalled as implicit in the preceding chapters of this present report.

Principle 1: The physical universe which mankind inhabits, like the creative powers of the human mind itself, contrary to the fraudulent myth of "zero economic growth," *is essentially premised on a negentropic principle of limitless development of the increased productive powers of labor, per capita and per square kilometer of territory.*

Principle 2: To a very large degree, mankind's limiting of its continued existence at any fixed, approximately habitual level of a fixed quality of skills, is entropic, and therefore morally, is also morally wrongful. The continued existence of human existence at any level of living population, depends upon an upward ordering of specifically anti-entropic changes in quality of behavior within societies.

Principle 3: The required anti-entropic action must reach to the level of a net increase of both the net physical productivity and the society's per-capita output measured in terms of human physical requirements. The principal correlative of that required increase, is typically expressed by the net increase of the ***energy-flux density*** of the action expressed as "power," per capita and per square-kilometer of the volume of the territory occupied by human existence. This is typified, for purposes of illustration, by progress from burning of trash, upward through the consumption of resources which are measured as such as charcoal, coal, coke, "natural gas," petroleum, controlled nuclear-fission, controlled thermonuclear fusion, and controlled "matter-anti-matter" reactions.

Principle 4: This requires a principle of devotion to the continuing increase in both the physical and cultural standard of living of the population, and the increase of the fruitful longevity of the population.

Principle 5: This requires the up-shift in the quality of human labor from relatively less dependency upon "human-physical" activity, to relatively more emphasis on "artificial" labor, as this development is expressed increasingly in the forms of advancing qualities of physical-scientific and Classical cultural modes of *physically productive* labor, that:

— as this principle of progress is already expressed in the effects of progressive modes of social organization typified by transition from modes of increasing per-capita energy-flux density, and, therefore, also capital intensity of the modes of productivity of societies.

—such as the transition from trans-oceanic, to inland riparian, to high-speed rail, and toward interplanetary modes of transport of human individuals and their products.

Man's progress depends upon mankind's wielding of increasingly greater and vaster forces than his own, reaching into the ranges of our Solar system, our galaxy, and the endless process of expanding and anti-entropically developing, our "finite but unbounded," universe as a whole.

Principle 6: The essential product of economy, presently, is the development of the quality of the human role in shaping the increasing portions of our planetary system (and beyond), as being increasingly, and efficiently, the habitat of mankind.

Principle 7: The appropriate price of goods, and related income, per capita and per square kilometer of surface territory, must be a fairly approximate reflection of those preceding six principles. Mankind exists in the image of the Creator of our universe, and has needs, and enjoys accomplishments, which reflect man as destined to live as if in the image of the Creator, as that presumption is also implicit in Soviet Academician V.I. Vernadsky's treatment of a universe composed of the three qualitative phases of *lithosphere*, *biosphere*, and *noösphere*.

That much said, within the just outlined context, now consider the necessary rules for the use of a system of money.

The Credit System

The foregoing physical-economic specifications define, implicitly, the methods which are required for leading the world successfully out of that presently on-rushing, global breakdown-crisis, a crisis which is currently approaching a terminal condition of general physical-economic life, in the form of a presently threatened, global, financial-monetary breakdown probably due, currently, for the interval of these present Summer months.

The functional relations within the economy, can not be competently defined in terms of separate categories as such, but must be defined as a complex, *dynamically*, according to Gottfried Leibniz's revolutionary 1690s definition of "dynamics," or, similarly, his revival, in this fashion, of the ancient Platonic notion of *dynamis* associated with the implications of Plato's **Parmenides** dialogue.

Therefore, the only competent mode of financial economy, is one defined by *a fixed-exchange-rate money-system*. This is required for *the internal discipline of a social economy of any sovereign nation-state*; it is also required among *a cooperating system of what are, respectively, perfectly sovereign nation-state economies*. However, a money system, even a fixed-exchange-rate system of money among nations, is not actually a determinant of economic "value," but is merely a kind of hypothetical bench-mark for estimating a measure of the actual, *only relative* progress of the national economic system as a whole.

The model form of reference for discussing the required national-economy system, is one which was rooted in the system of scrip which was developed as the system of credit which was associated with the Massachusetts Pinetree shilling, a practice which was continued for as long as Massachusetts retained its charter of sovereignty, prior to the British cancellation of that Massachusetts charter.

The principles implicit in the function of the sovereign Massachusetts system associated with the Pinetree shilling, would reappear in the prescriptions scheduled by the famous system of national banking established under U.S. Secretary of the Treasury Alexander Hamilton, a U.S. constitutional system which operated through the instrumentality of a sovereign system of national banking, that according to the same principle intended by the reforms of U.S. President Franklin Roosevelt, and also President Roosevelt's intended, "post-World War II" Bretton Woods establishment of a global fixed-exchange-rate system rooted in the same principles of national banking expressed by the Glass-Steagall Law.

The Meaning of Glass-Steagall

I repeat: in a sane economic system, money has no intrinsic value. It is not a proper measure of value, but in the nature of a bid on an adopted choice of contract. The corollary principle, is that of those who treat money as a useful estimate of a standard of relative price-value of production of goods and services.

The proper, actual choice of relative price-value is not located in the specific product or productive action as such, but in the product's relative value in the economic process of a nation, or of a group of sovereign nation-states considered as a dynamic whole—in Gott-

Tim Parkinson

"In a sane economic system, money has no intrinsic value." The role of the Pinetree shilling (left) in the Massachusetts Bay Colony of the 17th Century, was a model for a credit system, rather than a monetary system, such as we have today.

fried Leibniz's unique, original, 1690s, definition of the principle of the physical processes within the universe of an economy as a whole.

The social fact, that many people have been induced to regard money as a primary standard of value, shows, essentially, that they are the victims of what is admittedly a popular, and also often deadly form of delusion.

This does not mean that the proper choice of price lacks an element of reason. For example: if the price paid for production and distribution is relatively less, in cost of reproduction of that which is produced, the physical consequence will be attrition of the productive powers of labor. Thus, the targeted choice underlying a social system of pricing of produced goods and physically essential services, is located in the domain of rate of increase of the social-physical powers of reproduction in the functioning of society as *a physical-process-in-effect*.

That notion of physical effect, must be considered in the light of the seven principles of an anti-entropic physical system of economy as I have identified these seven, above. These considerations are, by the way, not-inconsistent with those implicitly presented in the core of U.S. Treasury Secretary Alexander Hamilton's treatment of **The Subject of Manufactures**.

The argument just developed so in this chapter thus far, is clarified by contrasting the American System of Economy with the predatory system of its hateful adversary, that British imperial system which obtained its roots from the irrationalist predatory character of the so-called "Liberal" dogma of Paolo Sarpi, and the Sarpi cult's follower Adam Smith.

I have, implicitly, addressed this subject earlier in

this present document; however, it is important, for practical purposes of the practice of economy, that the argument must be reconsidered, now, in the light of what has transpired within this report, thus far.

The Empire of Unreason

Since a certain time in Europe's history prior to the Peloponnesian War, the birth of European civilization in the form of an implicitly maritime-imperialist form of Mediterranean maritime culture, appeared chiefly as a reflection of the challenges represented by a then already ancient, earlier Egyptian civilization. The image of this development is reflected, as, for example, by the figure of Athena, in the contrasting sagas of the Homeric **Iliad** and **Odyssey**, and in Classical Greek literature referring to such a relationship. For the English reader, the celebrated work of genius presented by the clearly impassioned, most elegant translation met in **Chapman's Homer,** might be most pleasing to those who enjoy the style of performance, from behind the mask, of the dramas of Aeschylus.[31]

Something akin to the worst aspect of that ancient Greek maritime culture, is expressed in Aeschylus' **Prometheus** Trilogy, as the relevant view of the Olympian Zeus is presented as during Roman times by the Sicilian chronicler Diodorus Siculus. Aristotle speaks of this matter described by Aeschylus' **Prometheus** trilogy in Aristotle's own affinity for the notion of society in which "knowledge of the use of fire" (i.e., human creativity) is banned from the practice of the general, quasi-slave population under the reign of the Olympian style in oligarchy, as the legend of the Prometheus of Aeschylus presents this issue of social policy.[32]

The same issue, as the relevant issue of policy is affirmed by the enemy of Plato, Aristotle, is emphasized by the associate of the Christian Apostle Peter, Juda-

---

31. I refer here to my earlier remarks on the appropriate apprehension of the principles of drama.

32. Note, in particular, the pretense of British oligarchs to consider themselves in the likeness of the virtual pagan gods presented by Aeschylus, when compared to a more genial British population which is more largely induced to behave and think in a manner more appropriate to cattle, than to persons.

ism's Philo of Alexandria, who denounces Aristotle for claiming that the Creator lost the power to continue to create once an initial action of creation of the universe had been brought to a close. The exact same argument by Aristotle, is later expressed in Roman times in the disguise of the Aristotelean notions of *a-priorism* on which the Aristotelean geometry of Euclid had depended.

The Development of Man & Infrastructure

For reasons already delivered earlier since the outset of this present report, the need to prevent a natural decline of peoples and nations into depravity depends, as a matter of physical principle, on the increase of the productive powers of labor, per capita and per square kilometer. The preconditions for net progress of society depend primarily, on one part, on the advancement of the qualities associated with increase of the intellectual productive powers of labor and of what is conveniently termed "Classical culture," and on the quality of the basis represented by the qualitative development of basic economic infrastructure. The combined effect of those two crucial elements of progress is the increase of the power of the human species within the universe at large.

As I have developed the conception of the means by which the qualitative progress of the development of the human mind is attained, within the course of the preceding chapters of this present report, the continued success of mankind's performance as a species, depends upon a general shift in the notion of human nature, up from the relative bestiality of blind faith in what is called "sense certainty," to the notion of the wittingly, self-consciously creative individual personality who regards sense-perception and belief in the images of sense-certainty as the bestialized aspect of humanity's self-image. It is man and woman who recognize their identity and the power of our species as located essentially in a domain of creativity distinct from, and above notions of sense-certainty, as I have presented several images of that distinction within the preceding chapters of this report.

©Gert Mothes

Classical culture is a prerequisite for the development of the productive powers of labor, and thus for the increase of the power of the human species within the universe. Shown: The famed Thomanerchor *of Leipzig, Germany.*

With the advent of the discovery of the principle of the science of physical chemistry, that the proper universe of reference for physical science of economy is situated within the conception of a universe as essentially a domain of cosmic radiation, an image of man and woman appears to us as summarized in the celebrated first chapter of the Book of Genesis. With this step upward, we have entered the ante-room of the long-awaited discovery of the practical nature of the human species and its destiny.

It is, therefore, through the practiced awareness of this truer sense of the relationship of mankind among, and of the expanding universe, that the motives for a great advance in mankind's role in this universe now appear to us in a clear, scientific, and Classical cultural outlook.

This knowledge, and the devotion which it implies, must be the motive for the rise of mankind from the present state of a world now plunging, otherwise, into the greatest period of human depravity in the known social-intellectual history of mankind's past.

The document presented above, is the first of a series of reports intended to set forth, step by step, the new principles of world economy required for overcoming the epochal disaster represented by the onrushing collapse of the present world system.